Fourth Industrial Revolution: Reinvent or Perish

Fourth Industrial Revolution: Reinvent or Perish

Korean Conglomerates and Economy at the Crossroads

Seung Jin Kim

Copyright © 2024 Seung Jin Kim

All rights reserved.

ISBN: 9798333871336

Table of Contents

Preface 1

Chapter 1. Understanding the Role of Firms as the Engine of Economic Growth 7

Chapter 2. From the Miracle on the Han River to Growth Stagnation: The Journey of Korea's Economy 12

Chapter 3. The Dilemma of a Conglomerate-Centered Economy: Limitations Created by Success 30

3.1. Limitations of the Follower Growth Model 31

3.2. Limitations of High Market Concentration 42

Chapter 4. The Fourth Industrial Revolution: Waves of Change, Horizons of Possibility 49

4.1. A New Wave of Change 50

4.2. A New Horizon of Possibilities 103

Chapter 5. The Era of Great Transformation: A New Success Formula 110

Glossary 121

ABOUT THE AUTHOR 129

Preface

Dear readers,

Sixty years ago, South Korea was one of the poorest countries in the world. Today, it has grown into an advanced economy. At the heart of this remarkable journey were our companies. However, now this engine of growth is faltering. We face new challenges.

I am Seung Jin Kim. Through my diverse experiences as an economist, management consultant, and corporate executive, I've been able to observe in-depth the growth process of the Korean economy and corporate growth strategies. This book is the fruit of my efforts to share with you the insights and reflections gained from this process.

My journey began like this:

Starting as an Economist:
After receiving my Ph.D. in economics from University of Pennsylvania in the United States, I returned to Korea and worked as a researcher at a Korea's national think-tank KDI. During this period, I conducted numerous studies in the fields of industry and trade closely related to economic growth. Naturally, I became interested in Korean companies, but the view of companies through an economist's eyes was inevitably superficial. At the end of 1997, due to the foreign exchange crisis, Korea received IMF bailout funds and pursued corporate and financial sector restructuring led by the government. As a member of a national research institute, I participated in various research projects on Korea's economic situation and overcoming the foreign exchange crisis.

Transition to Management Consultant:
In the early 2000s, I moved to The Boston Consulting Group, a global management consulting firm, to better understand the reality of companies, and as a management consultant, I diagnosed companies and proposed solutions. The transformation from economist to management consultant was challenging, but it was a valuable experience in objectively understanding companies.

Experience as a Corporate Executive:

My experience, as a corporate executive and a president in Korea's large corporations, provided yet another perspective. While consulting firms mainly suggest ideas, companies carry out many implementations. I worked on establishing and executing strategies for large corporations, took responsibility for the operations of the entire global business, and took on the role of managing the business portfolio of an entire group.

This book has the following features:

1. This book takes a unique approach different from existing economic analyses or corporate research. Its main feature is viewing the economy through the lens of 'companies'. I believe that to understand a country's economy, one must look at its companies, and when examining its companies, one can see the country's economy. In particular, by studying Korea's large corporations, we can glimpse the future that the Korean economy will face.

2. In this book, particularly in Chapter 4, I have distilled the characteristics of the Fourth Industrial Revolution into three key aspects and elucidated them through ten comprehensive case studies. This approach reflects my endeavor as an author to dig into the essence of the Fourth Industrial Revolution. I am confident that this content will offer valuable insights to

global readers keen on grasping the core principles of this transformative era.

3. This book emphasizes the importance of 'Generative Innovation' in the context of the 4th Industrial Revolution. It goes beyond simply explaining technological changes to propose a fundamental paradigm shift. It stresses the importance of change and suggests directions for change.

4. This book is closer to an essay sharing thoughts based on personal experiences and observations rather than a research report. While it includes some data analysis, it primarily contains my personal observations, experiences, and the insights and thoughts derived from them. The messages in this book are entirely my personal perspectives and insights.

This book is structured as follows:

Chapter 1, 'Understanding the Role of Firms as the Engine of Economic Growth', examines the importance of firms in economic growth and the mechanisms for improving corporate productivity.

Chapter 2, 'From the Miracle on the Han River to Growth Stagnation: The Journey of the Korean Economy', analyzes the remarkable growth process of the Korean economy and the recent growth slowdown.

Chapter 3, 'The Dilemma of a Conglomerate-Centered Economy: Limitations Created by Success', discusses the pros and cons of the conglomerate-centered structure that has led Korea's economic growth and the challenges it currently faces.

Chapter 4, 'The 4th Industrial Revolution: Waves of Change, Horizons of Possibility', explores the technological changes brought by the 4th Industrial Revolution, the resulting changes in industrial structure, and the new opportunities and challenges given to companies. Specifically, it distills the characteristics of the Fourth Industrial Revolution into three key aspects. These are then elucidated through ten comprehensive case studies. This approach will provide readers with a deep understanding of the core principles of this transformative era.

Chapter 5, 'The Era of Great Transformation: A New Success Formula', proposes the direction Korean companies should take in the era of the 4th Industrial Revolution, the changes needed for this, and the role of the government.

Through this book, readers will be able to understand the current state of the Korean economy and contemplate together the direction that Korean companies and the economy should take in the era of the 4th Industrial Revolution.

I hope this book will serve as a platform to stimulate rich dialogue and discussion with readers. I hope it will help foster a true understanding of the economy and businesses, and that all readers will gain new insights through this book and find inspiration to apply to their work or thinking. Beyond simply providing information, I hope this book can contribute to expanding your thoughts and bringing about real change at a personal or organizational level. In this era of change, we are all looking for new paths to the future. I sincerely hope that this book will be of small help in that journey.

Chapter 1. Understanding the Role of Firms as the Engine of Economic Growth

In this chapter, we examine the role of firms as the core agent of the economy. We will explore how the economy works and what role firms play within it. In particular, we will look at how corporate productivity affects economic growth and how to increase productivity. Through this, we will understand why firms are the growth engine of the national economy.

To better understand the role of firms in the economy, it's essential to first grasp the broader economic context in which they operate.

The Economic Trio: Households, Firms, and Government

A country's economy operates through the interaction of three main agents: households, firms, and the government. Among these, firms hold a special position. Firms produce goods and services by inputting production factors such as labor and capital and sell these domestically or export them overseas. Additionally, firms support household consumption activities through compensation for labor input and carry out investment activities.

Their interaction can be simply expressed in the following equation:

GDP = Total Demand = Consumption + Investment + Government Spending + (Exports - Imports)

Here, GDP represents the total added value of goods and services produced domestically. The economy is in balance when GDP matches total demand.

The Key to Economic Growth: Firm Productivity

A country's economic growth refers to the process of GDP increasing while maintaining balance with total demand. Here, firms play a crucial role as the main producers. There are two ways for companies to increase production: increasing the input of production factors or improving productivity. Productivity refers to the ratio of output to input of production factors.

Simply put, it means how much value is created with the same number of resources. The higher the productivity, the more goods or services can be produced with fewer production factors.

The biggest role of firms in a country's economic growth lies in this increase in productivity. Why is that? If firms simply increase input of production factors without increasing productivity, economic growth will inevitably slow down. It becomes harder for firms to make more profits, and as a result, it becomes difficult to increase investment. Also, wage increases for workers are limited, making it difficult for household consumption to increase significantly. Moreover, production factors, especially labor force, cannot be supplied indefinitely. This is why many developed countries and some emerging countries are facing the problem of decreasing working-age population due to aging population.

Three Major Factors in Increasing Firm Productivity

How can firm productivity be increased? There are three major factors:

1. Research & Development:
Productivity can be increased through the development of new technologies or improvement of existing ones.

For example, automation technology can streamline the production process, allowing more products to be produced with fewer personnel. Also, the development of information and communication technology contributes to overall productivity improvement by enhancing internal communication and management systems within firms.

2. Human Capital:
This refers to the overall abilities and qualities of individuals, including education, training, and experience. Forming human capital requires a lot of time and resources, but it greatly contributes to productivity improvement through the development of new ideas and their application to actual production processes. For instance, highly skilled workers can produce more value in the same amount of time.

3. Economies of Scale:
This refers to the phenomenon where production costs per unit decrease as the scale of production increases. Large-scale production has several advantages. Fixed costs (e.g., R&D, facility investment) are spread over more products, reducing cost per unit, and raw material costs can be reduced through bulk purchasing. Also, labor productivity increases as tasks can be subdivided and employees can focus on specific tasks. In large-scale production, it becomes economically feasible to introduce expensive automated facilities, allowing more products to be produced within the same time.

Firms are the engine of economic growth, and improvements in firm productivity lead to economic growth.

Summary:

- ✓ **The economy operates through the interaction of households, firms, and the government.**
- ✓ **Firms play a key role in economic growth as the main producers.**
- ✓ **Improving firm productivity is the key to economic growth.**
- ✓ **Three major factors in improving firm productivity: R&D, human capital, economies of scale.**

Chapter 2. From the Miracle on the Han River to Growth Stagnation: The Journey of Korea's Economy

In this chapter, we will tell you the remarkable growth story of the Korean economy. We will examine how Korea, one of the world's poorest countries in the 1960s, leaped to become an economic powerhouse, and what challenges and crises it overcame in the process. We will also analyze in depth the causes and implications of the recent growth slowdown faced by the Korean economy.

Let's take a time machine back to the early 1960s. At that time, Korea's GDP per capita was lower than that of the Philippines. However, in just 60 years, Korea has come to be recognized as an advanced economy. How was this possible?

The Remarkable Growth of the Korean Economy

UNCTAD, a UN body, classified Korea from a developing country to a developed country in 2021. This was the first case of reclassifying a developing country to a developed country since UNCTAD's establishment in 1964, once again confirming the remarkable development of the Korean economy.

International organizations use different criteria to classify countries' development stages. Korea was classified as a High-income Country by the World Bank and an Advanced Economy by the IMF in the mid-1990s. Korea joined the OECD in 1996, and in 2019, it voluntarily gave up its developing country status in the WTO, indicating its willingness to no longer request preferential treatment as a developing country. With UNCTAD reclassifying Korea as a developed country, Korea is now recognized as a developed economy by all major international organizations.

The numbers showing this change are truly astonishing.

In the early 1960s, Korea's GDP per capita was very low by global standards. In 1961, Korea's GDP per capita was $1,066, which was more than three times lower than the world average of $3,685, and even lower than the Philippines' $1,129.

<Table 1> GDP per capita, US$, 1961

Country	1961
Korea	1,066
Philippines	1,129
Japan	6,952
United States	19,253
World	3,685

Source World Bank
Note: Based on 2015 prices

About 60 years later, the situation has completely changed. In 2022, Korea's GDP per capita reached $33,719, which is about three times higher than the world average of $11,315, and on par with Japan.

<Table 2> GDP per capita, US$, 2022

Country	2022
Korea	33,719
Philippine	3,528
Japan	36,202
United States	62,789
World	11,315

Source: World Bank
Note: Based on 2015 prices

Between 1961 and 2022, Korea's GDP per capita increased about 32-fold. Compared to the world average which tripled during the same period, this is truly remarkable growth. Japan increased 5-fold, the U.S. 3-fold, and the Philippines 3-fold.

<Figure 1> GDP per capita, US$, 1961, 2022

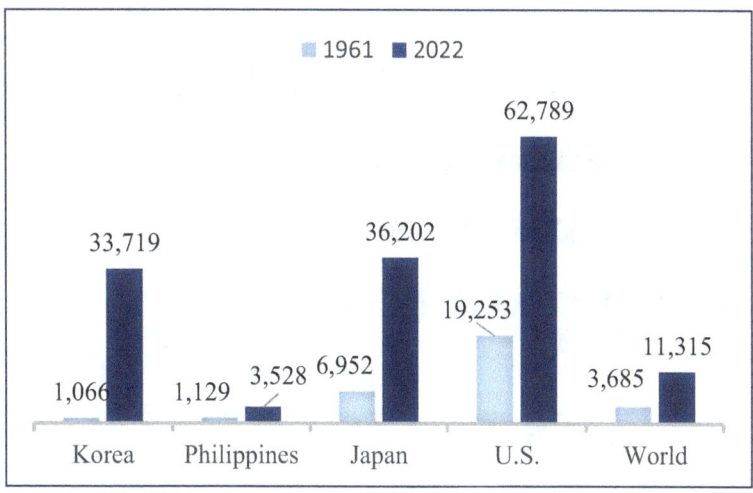

Source: World Bank
Note: Based on 2015 prices

The Korean economy has experienced solid economic growth over the past 60 years to reach the income level of developed countries. From 1961 to 2022, Korea recorded remarkably high growth rates globally, with a CAGR (Compound Annual Growth Rate) of GDP at 7.04% during this period, more than double the world's overall GDP growth rate. It's hard to find a country with a higher GDP CAGR than Korea during this period other than China (8.45%), indicating that Korea's economic growth has been very successful.

<Figure 2> GDP Growth Rate, %, CAGR, 1961~2022

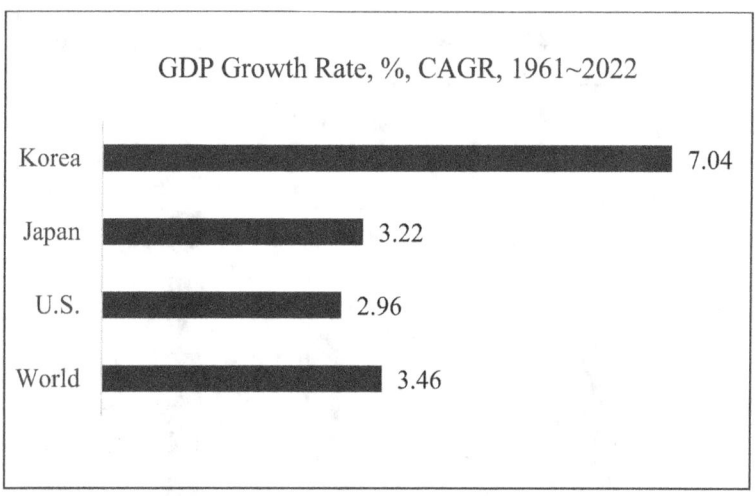

Source: World Bank

Slowdown in Korea's Economic Growth

Korea's economic growth is on a downward trend. The Korean economy showed high growth from the early stages of economic development until the mid-1990s, recorded relatively good growth until the mid-2000s after the foreign exchange crisis, and has been showing a low growth trend since the global financial crisis.

1961~1997

The Korean economy grew rapidly from the early 1960s to 1997. Korea recorded a compound annual growth rate (CAGR) of GDP at 9.38% from 1961 to 1997, which far exceeded the world's overall GDP growth rate of 3.81% during the same period.

<Table 3> GDP Growth Rate, CAGR, %, 1961~1997

Country	1961~1997
Korea	9.38
Japan	5.12
United States	3.47
World	3.81

Source: World Bank

The 1960s-1970s was a period of ultra-high economic growth performance due to the government-led economic development plan, and the Korean economy continued its rapid growth until the mid-1990s. Korea's economic growth was evaluated as a successful case to the extent that it was called the Asian Miracle, and it also became a benchmarking target for many developing countries.

Foreign Exchange Crisis

However, the growth process was not always smooth. At the end of 1997, Korea faced a major crisis called the foreign exchange crisis.

Korean firms and financial institutions were increasing short-term foreign currency borrowing with low interest rates for financing, but in this process, firms' profitability significantly decreased due to indiscriminate business expansion, and financial institutions' burden of repaying foreign currency borrowing greatly increased as bad loans surged. As foreigners withdrew funds from the Korean market and foreign exchange reserves rapidly decreased, the value of the Korean currency (won) plummeted in the foreign exchange market. Several large corporations went bankrupt in succession, and as external confidence in the Korean financial market further deteriorated, Korea's foreign exchange reserves were depleted.

In December 1997, the Korean government requested a bailout from the IMF, and the IMF provided about $58 billion in emergency funds while demanding strict reforms in the financial and corporate sectors. Of this amount, the IMF directly contributed $21 billion, while the remaining $37 billion was arranged by the IMF from other sources such as the World Bank, Asian Development Bank, and individual countries. Accordingly, the Korean government carried out massive restructuring in the financial and corporate sectors. In this process, many corporations and financial institutions were merged or liquidated.

Korea's GDP decreased significantly, and unemployment rate soared.

As a result, the Korean economy recorded negative growth in 1998. The foreign exchange crisis had a huge impact on the Korean economy, with GDP growth rate recording -5.13% in 1998.

<Table 4> GDP Growth Rate, %, 1998

Country	1998
Korea	-5.13
Japan	-1.27
Germany	2.01
United States	4.48
World	2.86

Source: World Bank

However, the Korean economy showed remarkable resilience. It overcame the crisis through intense restructuring and reforms and regained high growth from 1999.

1999~2007

The Korean economy recorded relatively good growth from 1999 to 2007. Korea recorded a CAGR of GDP at 5.65% from 1999 to 2007, which exceeded the world's overall GDP growth rate of 3.65% during the same period.

<Table 5> GDP Growth Rate, CAGR, %, 1999~2007

Country	1999~2007
Korea	5.65
Japan	1.44
Germany	1.54
United States	2.70
World	3.65

Source: World Bank

The world economy recorded good growth again after the collapse of the dot-com bubble (an event where internet firm stock prices rose sharply and then plummeted) in 2000. In particular, emerging market economies like China and India grew rapidly, international trade and capital flows increased, and the real estate markets of major countries like the U.S. boomed based on low interest rates and innovative financial products.

After 1999, the Korean economy grew rapidly centered on exports. Conglomerates grew significantly in the global market of major manufacturing industries such as semiconductors, automobiles, and electronics, which was attributed to conglomerates being reorganized into more efficient structures during the corporate restructuring process. In particular, some conglomerates like Samsung and LG came to play a leading role in the global market through massive investments in technology development.

Global Financial Crisis

The financial crisis that started in the U.S. in 2007~8 swept the world.

In the U.S.., large-scale high-risk mortgage loans, known as subprime mortgage loans, were made to borrowers with low credit ratings, where default problems occurred. Subprime mortgage loans were packaged into complex derivative financial products and sold to financial institutions worldwide, but many investors and financial institutions failed to properly recognize the risks of these products.

As financial market instability began in 2007, several subprime mortgage companies went bankrupt, and in 2008, the large investment bank Lehman Brothers went bankrupt. The U.S. government provided bailouts to financial institutions to stabilize the financial market, implemented interest rate cuts and quantitative easing, and greatly expanded fiscal spending to stimulate the economy.

The financial crisis that occurred in the U.S. spread to Europe, Asia, etc. In Europe, many banks had invested in high-risk mortgage securities in the U.S., and the losses incurred from this caused a huge shock to the banking system across Europe. European governments supplied liquidity to the market through interest rate cuts and quantitative easing to stabilize the financial market and expanded fiscal spending to stimulate the economy. Asian economies were also affected by the financial crisis, but not as severely as the U.S. or Europe. However, countries with high export dependence were greatly affected by the decrease in global demand.

The global financial crisis had a tremendous impact on the world economy. Many countries, including the U.S., experienced economic recessions, leading to rising unemployment rates and sharp declines in investment and consumption.

<Table 6> GDP Growth Rate, %, 2008, 2009

Country	2008	2009
Korea	3.01	0.79
Japan	-1.22	-5.70
Germany	0.96	-5.69
United States	0.12	-2.60
World	2.06	-1.36

Source: World Bank

Before the financial crisis, from 1999 to 2007, the world economy recorded a relatively good annual average growth rate of about 3.65%, but in 2008 the growth rate dropped significantly, and in 2009 it recorded a negative growth rate.

Immediately after the global financial crisis, as the world economy entered a recession phase, the Korean economy also experienced difficulties. Korean financial institutions had relatively little exposure to high-risk mortgage securities, so direct losses were not significant. However, as demand in major export markets such as the U.S. and Europe significantly decreased, Korea's exports greatly decreased. As a result, Korea's economic growth rate plummeted to 0.79% in 2009.

2010~2022

Thanks to stimulus measures and economic recovery efforts in countries around the world, the world economy showed a recovery in growth rate from 2010, but the growth rate slowed compared to the early to mid-2000s. Many European countries still struggled with economic growth due to serious debt problems, and the growth rate of international trade also decreased due to factors such as the U.S.-China trade war. Along with this, structural factors such as population aging also affected the slowdown in world economic growth. The world economic growth rate from 2010 to 2022 recorded an annual average of 2.75%, which shows a clear slowdown compared to the average of 3.65% from 1999 to 2007.

<Table 7> GDP Growth Rate, CAGR, %, 2010~2022

Country	2010~2022
Korea	2.72
Japan	0.59
Germany	1.37
United States	2.06
World	2.75

Source: World Bank

During this period, the economic growth rates of major countries in the world slowed down. The economic growth rates of major developed countries such as the U.S., Germany, and Japan mostly decreased. Korea's economic growth rate also decreased.

In particular, Korea's economic growth has slowed rapidly in recent years. Comparing the compound annual growth rate (CAGR) of GDP between 1999-2007 and 2010-2022, Korea's GDP growth rate sharply dropped from 5.65% to 2.72%.

\<Figure 3\> Difference from World GDP Growth Rate, %, 1999~2007, 2010~2022

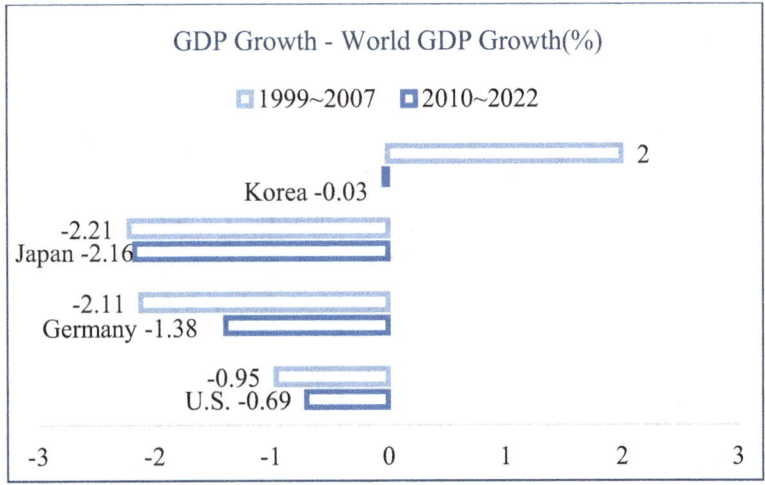

Source: World Bank

Korea's GDP growth rate was 2% higher than the world GDP growth rate of 3.65% in 1999-2007, but in 2010-2022, it recorded a level slightly below the world GDP growth rate of 2.75%. In contrast, developed countries such as Japan, Germany, and the U.S. recorded lower levels than the world GDP growth rate in 1999-2007, but in 2010-2022, they showed a narrowing gap with the world GDP growth rate.

The significant slowdown in Korea's GDP growth was closely related to the deceleration in export growth and the sluggish performance of the service industry.

Let's look at more details.

Export Growth Slowdown

Korea's export share in the economy has been very high. Korea's export share to GDP is at the level of 47-48%, which is much higher than major countries such as Japan and the United States, and similar to Germany.

<Table 8> Export Share to GDP, %, 2010, 2022

Country	2010	2022
Korea	47.1	48.2
Japan	14.9	21.5
Germany	42.6	50.9
United States	12.3	11.8
World	28.7	31.1

Source: World Bank

Korea's export growth rate has significantly slowed down. Comparing the compound annual average export growth rates between 1999-2007 and 2010-2022, Korea's export growth rate dropped significantly from 11.71% to 4.01%. Korea's export growth rate was almost twice as high as the world export growth rate of 6.51% in 1999-2007, but it dropped significantly to a level close to the world export growth rate of 3.17% in 2010-2022.

<Table 9> Export Growth Rate, CAGR, %, 1999~2007, 2010~2022

Country	1999~2007	2010~2022
Korea	11.71	4.01
Japan	7.87	2.29
Germany	8.05	3.07
United States	4.57	2.07
World	6.51	3.17

Source: World Bank

Poor Growth in Service Industry

Korea's service industry share in GDP is remarkably low compared to other major economies. As of 2022, the service industry value-added share to GDP in Korea stands at approximately 58%, which is significantly lower than advanced economies such as the United States, Japan, and Germany. Surprisingly, it even falls below the world average. This statistic is particularly striking given Korea's overall economic development.

This indicates that Korea's service industry is relatively underdeveloped in comparison to other countries, but it also means that Korea's service industry has great growth potential.

<Table 10> Service Industry Value-Added to GDP, %, 2010, 2022

Country	2010	2022
Korea	54.7	58.0
Japan	70.5	71.4
Germany	62.3	62.7
United States	76.3	77.6 (2021)
World	62.8	61.7

Source: World Bank
Note: The 2022 data for the U.S. is not available.

Korea's service industry is steadily growing, but it's hard to say it's fast enough to trigger economic growth. Comparing the annual average value-added growth rates between 1999-2007 and 2010-2022, the decline in the service industry value-added growth rate was relatively smaller than that of the manufacturing industry, and as a result, it now slightly exceeds the growth rate of the manufacturing industry. However, it's not yet sufficient to act as a new growth engine driving Korea's economic growth.

<Table 11> Value-Added Growth Rate, CAGR, %, 1999~2007, 2010~2022

Industry	1999~2007	2010~2022
Manufacturing	8.09	2.69
Service	5.36	3.08

Source: World Bank

Summary:

- ✓ **The Korean economy achieved advanced country income levels in 60 years.**
- ✓ **It achieved very rapid economic growth from the 1960s to 1997.**
- ✓ **After overcoming the foreign exchange crisis, it maintained solid growth until the mid-2000s.**
- ✓ **After the global financial crisis in 2007-8, it shifted to a low growth trend.**
- ✓ **Korea's economic growth slowed down relatively rapidly.**

Chapter 3. The Dilemma of a Conglomerate-Centered Economy: Limitations Created by Success

In this chapter, we will examine how the conglomerate-centered economic structure, which forms the foundation of the Korean economy, was formed, and what limitations it is currently facing. We will focus on analyzing competition in the global market and productivity issues in the domestic service sector and look at how these structural problems affect the Korean economy.

As mentioned in Chapter 2, Korea's economic growth has slowed significantly in recent years. The main reasons cited were the slowdown in export growth and poor growth in the service sector. Now, it's time to ask a more fundamental question.

What are the root causes of the slowdown in export growth and poor growth in the service sector?

3.1. Limitations of the Follower Growth Model

The secret to South Korea's rapid economic growth over the past few decades was its conglomerate-centered economic structure. From the early stages of economic growth until now, conglomerates have not only accounted for a very large proportion of the Korean economy but have also exerted absolute influence when considering their associated effects. In particular, the proportion of conglomerates in exports is overwhelming.

The reason why the government intensively supported conglomerates from the beginning is closely related to economic growth through export expansion. The conglomerate system had strengths in rapidly pioneering overseas markets and increasing exports in a short period of time. Based on government support, conglomerates achieved high market shares in the domestic market and grew rapidly in overseas markets by leveraging economies of scale to lead in price competitiveness. Although they lacked technological prowess compared to global leading companies, they quickly improved quality and performance through technology adoption and development, and rapidly increased exports and overseas sales by leveraging the advantage of low prices compared to quality and performance.

However, entering the 1990s, concerns about the so-called 'nutcracker' phenomenon grew. The 'nutcracker' phenomenon refers to the situation where Korea is struggling between developed countries and developing countries. This phenomenon describes the situation where Korea is having difficulty narrowing the technology gap with developed countries while simultaneously losing competitiveness due to the rapid pursuit of late-developing countries. As concerns grew that Korea's manufacturing industry could lose competitiveness in the global market due to lower technological prowess compared to Japan and lower price competitiveness compared to China, there were many points that Korea's manufacturing industry needed a breakthrough to continue growing in the global market.

In this regard, I am reminded of the words of Kim Woo-Joong, Chairman of Daewoo Group, around 1997. At the time, Daewoo Group was pursuing 'global management' and expanding its business in several countries. In particular, it was pursuing aggressive investment and market development targeting emerging countries such as Eastern Europe and Central Asia. Chairman Kim said:

"It's true that Korean companies lag behind advanced country companies in technology. We also need to strengthen technology development, but it will take time. Daewoo's global management is a strategy to preempt emerging markets. We will expand market entry as a package centered on automobiles, including electronics and construction. We will strengthen insufficient technology by establishing R&D bases in advanced countries."

This statement can be interpreted as follows:
"We grew rapidly with price competitiveness compared to quality, but this alone makes it difficult to grow as a major player in global competition. We need a new breakthrough. Since it takes a long time to catch up with advanced companies in technology, we are trying to establish overseas bases first to preempt and expand emerging markets."

In retrospect, Daewoo Group's 'global management' was a strategic choice for continued growth in the global market. Although it ultimately failed due to the overlap of debt from business expansion and the foreign exchange crisis, it can be seen as an attempt made as a breakthrough for growth in global competition.

After the foreign exchange crisis at the end of 1997, many conglomerates underwent restructuring and actively pursued technology development investment and global market expansion. At that time, conglomerates chose one of two major strategies:

1. Technology Focus Strategy: A strategy to expand the global market with top-level technological capabilities

2. Market Focus Strategy: A strategy that prioritizes global market development or network expansion while gradually improving technology (similar to the Daewoo Group case mentioned earlier)

Technology Focus Strategy

As a result of actively investing in technology development from a long-term perspective, some conglomerates rose to the position of leaders with top-level technological capabilities in the global market around 2010.

Looking at representative fields:

Semiconductors: Samsung Electronics is leading the world in both technological prowess and market share in the DRAM market and NAND flash memory market.

Smartphones: Samsung Electronics, along with Apple, is leading the global smartphone market and is recognized for its technological prowess with innovative features and high-quality products.

OLED TV panels: LG Display boasts an overwhelming market share and world-class technological capabilities.

Electric vehicle batteries: LG Energy Solution and Samsung SDI maintain top positions in the global market with world-class technological capabilities.

In this way, some conglomerates such as Samsung and LG have leaped to become global leaders in their main business areas through bold and active investment in technology development.

Market Focus Strategy

On the other hand, many conglomerates chose a strategy of prioritizing global market expansion while gradually improving technology. They still remain in a follower position, with a technology gap compared to leader companies in the global market.

After the 2007-2008 global financial crisis, the world economy showed recovery from 2010, but growth slowed down, and this trend continues. As a result, Korean conglomerates have faced difficulties in growing in the global market, and export growth has also significantly slowed.

When market growth is good, both leaders and followers can grow easily. However, when market growth slows or stagnates, leaders struggle, but followers are hit harder. Leaders have a solid loyal customer base due to brand strength and have an advantage in price competition with high margins. On the other hand, followers lack brand power and loyal customer base, and find it difficult to respond to price competition due to low margins.

In particular, Korean conglomerate followers face greater difficulties when global demand slows down. The decrease in production and sales due to global demand slowdown weakens the effect of economies of scale, hindering productivity improvement. They have high fixed costs, making it difficult to reduce costs when demand decreases, worsening profitability. If price competition becomes fierce due to market share competition, they face additional profitability pressure.

Ultimately, conglomerate followers have a structure that is very vulnerable to global market slowdown because they have relied on economies of scale to increase productivity.

With many conglomerates or large corporations affiliated with conglomerate groups still in a follower position in the global market, the recent sharp slowdown in Korean exports shows the limitations of this follower growth model.

The bigger problem is that the slowdown in world economic growth is likely to continue in the future. The World Bank predicts that the world's potential GDP growth rate (annual average) for 2022-2030 will fall to 2.2%, the lowest level in the past 30 years. This means that almost all factors that contributed to world economic growth are disappearing. For example, labor supply is decreasing due to population aging in many developed countries and some emerging countries, and world trade growth is slowing down due to trade barriers and other factors.

**World potential GDP growth rate: The maximum growth rate at which the world economy can grow without causing inflation

If the slowdown in world economic growth becomes prolonged, many large corporations affiliated with conglomerate groups will inevitably struggle to grow in the global market. This can cause a chain of difficulties in the production and exports of SMEs (small and medium-sized enterprises) linked to large corporations. Considering that a significant number of rapidly growing SMEs in Korea are linked to large corporations, the difficulties of large corporations can pose a risk of spreading to the entire economy.

If conglomerate followers could rise to the position of leaders with global top-level technology, these impacts could be minimized, but the possibility seems very low at present. To become a leader, you need to take high risks and make huge investments. Many conglomerate followers are making significant investments in R&D, but they have tended to focus on short-term cost reduction and rapid profit generation. It can be seen that they focused on improving existing technology rather than making huge investments with high risks over a long period.

Most conglomerates already have high market dominance in the domestic market in their main manufacturing sectors. Based on this, they were able to generate stable profits and achieve aggressive growth in overseas markets. In particular, despite being far from global top-level technology, conglomerate followers were able to achieve both stable profits and growth through domestic market dominance and price competitiveness in overseas markets. Conglomerates' market dominance in the domestic manufacturing market is still high, and the domestic market plays an important role as a stable source of revenue for conglomerates.

In addition, Korean conglomerates are securing another stable source of revenue by conducting various businesses in the domestic service industry market. This diversification strategy helps them to mitigate risks associated with their main manufacturing sectors.

Generally, a company can grow by focusing on one field or by entering various fields. Companies constantly pursue ways to grow in their main field but also seek diversification by entering new businesses. However, there are not many cases of diversifying into as many business areas as Korean conglomerates. Large corporations in the U.S. or Europe also diversify their businesses, but in most cases, they selectively enter related fields centered on their main areas. In Japan, there are *keiretsu* that refer to large groups, which tend to concentrate relatively within specific industries and have a weaker degree of diversification compared to Korean large business groups.

Is it because developed countries have large domestic markets in one field that companies can grow by specializing in one field, while Korea had to diversify into various fields because it's not like that? In the era of global competition, if there is a technological advantage, growth can be achieved through overseas market expansion beyond the domestic market. Of course, we can't say there's no home advantage, but we see many global companies growing in overseas markets. Isn't the fact that Korean conglomerates' business diversification is more prominent than large business groups in developed countries related to the fact that many conglomerates don't have technological advantages in their main fields?

Looking at the growth process of many Korean conglomerates, they started with technology introduction initially and are actively investing in technology development afterwards, but it's closer to improving existing technology rather than developing new technology. Many large corporations affiliated with conglomerate groups have a technology gap with leading companies in developed countries. In a situation where there is no solid technological advantage in global competition, diversifying into various business fields in the domestic market, especially the service industry, has become a relatively safe and effective way to expand revenue sources.

Looking at the business portfolio of conglomerate groups, even if there are fields competing globally, there are many cases of entering various service industry fields such as distribution, finance, IT, and leisure targeting domestic demand. There are also cases where they focused only on the domestic market without global competition, increasing market dominance or diversifying businesses.

Conglomerate groups generally generate stable profits with high market dominance in the domestic market in their main fields. In addition to this, securing stable revenue sources in various fields of the service industry could be an attractive strategic option for them. Conglomerate groups were able to generate stable profits domestically by utilizing various business networks already established in the domestic market. From the perspective of conglomerate groups, unlike competing in the global market, they have an advantage over foreign companies in the domestic service industry market due to various regulations or practices, and have an advantage over small and medium-sized enterprises or new companies due to differences in capital power and business networks.

As a result, many conglomerates were able to secure stable revenue sources through high market share in the domestic market and business diversification. This enables them to achieve growth based on price competitiveness in overseas markets. Even if there was a technology gap with leaders in the global market, it was possible to achieve sufficiently stable profits and growth for the group as a whole. In this situation, can conglomerates make long-term massive technology development investments to rise to the position of leaders with global top-level technology? In a situation where stable profits are secured through highly concentrated structures in the domestic market, the possibility of making investments that require large-scale funds and involve risks is not high.

Then, is there a possibility that SMEs will provide new momentum for Korea's export growth? I think it's very unlikely to happen at present. A considerable number of SMEs are still strongly linked to large corporations affiliated with conglomerate groups, and the proportion of SMEs exporting independently is not yet sufficient.

3.2. Limitations of High Market Concentration

As explained earlier, many large corporations, in the form of conglomerates, have high market dominance not only in manufacturing but also in domestic service industries. In various domestic service sectors such as finance, distribution, telecommunications, logistics, IT services, advertising, and marketing, almost all of the top three companies in terms of market share are affiliated with large conglomerates.

Large conglomerates have expanded their business scope in the domestic service market by leveraging their existing market dominance and business networks. They held a much more advantageous position in terms of capital and business networks compared to small and medium-sized enterprises, and enjoyed an advantage in entering the domestic market over foreign companies due to home market advantages.

The problem is that this structure keeps the productivity of domestic service industries at a very low level. Specifically:

1. Low productivity compared to manufacturing:

The productivity of domestic service industries is less than 60% of manufacturing productivity based on value-added per worker. In contrast, in other developed countries, service industry productivity is similar to or even higher than manufacturing. For example, in Germany and Japan, service industry productivity is 80-90% of manufacturing, and in the US, it exceeds 100%.

2. Significantly low level in international comparison:

The productivity of domestic service industries is only 77% of Japan's, 67% of Germany's, and 39% of the United States' based on value-added per worker.

(When comparing productivity based on value-added per working hour, considering that Korean workers' average working hours are relatively high, the productivity gap could be even larger.)

<Table 12> Value-Added per Worker, US$, 2022

Country	Service	Manufacturing
Korea	49,636	83,925
Japan	64,393	85,515
Germany	73,867	83,525
U.S.	127,772	122,304

Source: World Bank
Note: Based on 2015 prices

3. Slow productivity growth:

The rate of increase in service industry productivity is not fast enough to affect the overall productivity growth of domestic industries.

<Table 13> Growth Rate of Value-Added per Worker, CAGR, %, 1999~2007, 2010~2022

Country	Service 1999~2007	Service 2010~2022	Manufacturing 1999~2007	Manufacturing 2010~2022
Korea	2.23	1.62	5.83	1.24
Japan	0.82	-0.28	2.74	0.98
Germany	0.43	0.37	2.54	0.92
U.S.	1.51	1.02	1.76	0.72

Source: World Bank

This low productivity limits the growth of the service industry. Low productivity weakens investment incentives and makes it difficult to meet the increasing demand for services that comes with economic development.

Of course, many point out that regulations related to the service industry are a problem. There have been policy efforts to ease service industry regulations, but it's true that they are insufficient from a business perspective, and these efforts need to be redoubled.

The more fundamental problem is the lack of competition. It can be seen that large corporations maintaining high market dominance in the domestic service market based on powerful capital and strong business-related networks has acted as a cause of low productivity in domestic service industries. When a few companies dominate the market, price or service quality competition is limited, and there is not enough incentive to improve productivity through innovation. If the competitive pressure is large enough for large corporations affiliated with conglomerates to feel threatened in maintaining their dominance in the domestic service market, they will have to be more proactive in improving productivity.

Recalling the research, I did at a national research institute in the early 2000s, Foreign Direct Investment (FDI) had a direct effect on increasing the productivity of domestic industries. Empirical analysis showed that the productivity of FDI firms entering Korea was higher than that of domestic firms. What I paid more attention to was the indirect effect of FDI increasing the productivity of domestic industries. My thought at the time was that FDI firms could increase the productivity of large corporations dominating the domestic market by increasing competition in the domestic market. I thought that to mitigate the problem of limited competition due to the concentration of economic power by conglomerates, an increase in competitive pressure was needed, and FDI firms entering the domestic market could practically play this role. At that time, FDI inflow was not large compared to the size of the Korean economy, and I anticipated that if FDI inflow were to increase, the indirect productivity increase effect would potentially become larger. The reason I recalled my research from long ago, is to emphasize the importance of competition for increasing productivity in domestic service industries.

In the current situation, can large corporations affiliated with conglomerates lead the improvement of productivity in domestic service industries?

I doubt whether they have sufficient incentives to lead the improvement of productivity in the domestic service market where their dominance is high, as it is.

Then, can small and medium-sized enterprises contribute more to increasing service industry productivity? That possibility seems low. This is because the productivity of small and medium-sized enterprises in domestic service industries is much lower than that of large corporations.

We reach the following conclusion:

If the slowdown in world economic growth becomes prolonged, a slowdown in Korea's export growth is inevitable. If the productivity of domestic service industries continues to remain at a low level, it will be difficult for the service industry to become a new driver of economic growth.

Korea achieved rapid economic growth in the past by relying on a conglomerate-centered economic structure, but this structure clearly has limitations in bringing sustainable economic growth in the future.

Summary:

- ✓ The conglomerate-centered economic structure was the driving force of Korea's economic growth.
- ✓ Many large corporations affiliated with conglomerates are still in a follower position in the global market.
- ✓ The export-led growth model of conglomerates has faced limitations due to the slowdown in global economic growth.
- ✓ The low productivity of domestic service industries makes it difficult to create new growth engines.
- ✓ The high market dominance of conglomerates is hindering innovation and productivity improvement in the service industry.

Now we face a new challenge. How can we overcome these limitations and find new growth engines? In the next chapter, we will explore the new opportunities and challenges offered by the Fourth Industrial Revolution.

Chapter 4. The Fourth Industrial Revolution: Waves of Change, Horizons of Possibility

We now stand before a massive wave of change. Shall we explore together the revolutionary changes that the Fourth Industrial Revolution will bring and the opportunities hidden within it? In this chapter, we will predict how the convergence of various technologies creates new business models and innovative solutions, and how this will change industrial structures and competitive landscapes.

In Chapter 3, I mentioned that Korea's economic growth slowdown stems from the limitations of its conglomerate-centered economic structure. There is little chance that this structure, which has been maintained and strengthened for decades, will change in a short period. Therefore, whether conglomerates can find new growth engines will determine the future of the Korean economy.

I focus on the changes and possibilities that the Fourth Industrial Revolution will bring. Let's examine this step by step.

4.1. A New Wave of Change

First, let's briefly define what the Fourth Industrial Revolution is. The World Economic Forum (WEF) explains it like this:

"The Fourth Industrial Revolution is a technological innovation that fuses the physical, digital, and biological worlds. Advanced technologies such as artificial intelligence (AI), robotics, the Internet of Things (IoT), and 3D printing are causing major changes across industries and having a significant impact on social and economic structures. This includes improvements in productivity, the creation of new business models, changes in employment, and more."

To help you understand, I'll briefly explain the key technologies of the Fourth Industrial Revolution:

1. Artificial Intelligence (AI): Computer systems that mimic or surpass human intelligence

2. Big Data: Technology to analyze vast amounts of data and extract valuable information

3. Internet of Things (IoT): Technology to connect all things via the internet to exchange information

4. 5G: Next-generation communication technology characterized by ultra-high speed, ultra-low latency, and hyper-connectivity

5. Cloud Computing: Technology that provides computing resources via the internet

6. Blockchain: Distributed data storage technology that ensures data security and transparency

7. AR/VR: Technology that adds virtual information to reality (AR) or creates a completely virtual environment (VR)

8. Robotics: Technology to develop automated machines and systems

9. Biotechnology: Technology to create products or improve processes using biological systems

10. 3D Printing: Technology to create objects based on three-dimensional design data

In the history of industrial revolutions, there have already been the First, Second, and Third Industrial Revolutions. These industrial revolutions brought about significant technological advancements and social changes.

The First Industrial Revolution, spanning from the late 18th to the early 19th century, was marked by the invention of the steam engine and the rise of mechanized production facilities. This period saw the emergence of mass production using machines, the development of the manufacturing industry, and the introduction of new transportation methods such as railways.

The Second Industrial Revolution, occurring from the late 19th to the early 20th century, was defined by the widespread use of electricity, the invention of the internal combustion engine, and the introduction of the assembly line (Ford system). These innovations led to significant productivity improvements through the use of electrical energy, the establishment of large-scale factory production systems, and the emergence of new communication means like telephones and radios, as well as new forms of transportation such as automobiles.

The Third Industrial Revolution, extending from the late 20th to the early 21st century, was characterized by the advent of computers and the Internet. This phase brought about innovation in information processing and sharing through the digitalization of information, leading to the emergence of new industries such as IT and communication.

So, how is the Fourth Industrial Revolution different from previous Industrial Revolutions?

Let me introduce the differences I see:

(1) Various technologies can be integrated or converged.

(2) Through the convergence of technologies, it's possible to create customer-centric innovative solutions.

(3) Industrial structures and competitive landscapes change rapidly.

These three differences I have outlined are not merely distinctions from previous revolutions. In fact, they constitute the very essence of the Fourth Industrial Revolution. These key characteristics define its transformative nature and fundamentally set it apart as a truly revolutionary era.

Let's look at these three points in detail. For each point, I will explain what it means and how it can be possible, using examples or cases to illustrate.

<Figure 4> Characteristics of the Fourth Industrial Revolution

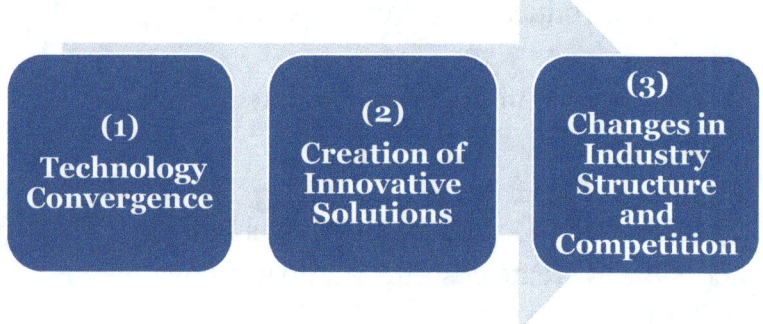

(1) Convergence of Various Technologies

Core: AI + Big Data

The core of the Fourth Industrial Revolution is the convergence of artificial intelligence and big data. These two technologies work closely together in the process of data collection, transmission, storage, analysis, learning, and execution. For example, when big data technology collects data from various sources, artificial intelligence analyzes it to learn patterns and generate models. The AI models created in this way analyze data in real-time in actual business environments and provide solutions.

To help you understand, I'll explain the integration process of these two technologies in more detail.

Data Collection Stage:
Big data technology is used to collect data from various sources (e.g., websites, social media, transaction records).

Data Transmission and Storage Stage:
The collected data is transmitted to data centers via the internet. Big data technology is used to store data in a distributed manner, with structured and unstructured data stored in separate databases. Big data technology is used to refine the data, correcting errors and converting it into a form suitable for analysis.

Data Analysis and Learning Stage:
Big data technology is used to analyze data and extract important features. Artificial intelligence (machine learning/deep learning algorithms) analyzes the relationships between the extracted features to learn patterns, thereby generating AI models. The generated

AI models improve their performance through continuous learning, are then saved as files, and are deployed to On-Premise Servers for use in actual business environments.

*Machine Learning Algorithm: A methodology that uses data to learn patterns and performs prediction, classification, clustering, etc. for new data based on learned patterns.
*Deep Learning Algorithm: A subfield of machine learning, a methodology that can learn and process more complex and high-dimensional patterns.
*On-Premise Server: A physical server located within an organization.

Execution Stage:
In actual business environments, AI models analyze data in real-time to provide various solutions. Big data technology continuously collects new data, and artificial intelligence improves models through this.

Without big data technology, it would be virtually impossible to create artificial intelligence. In AI, machine learning and deep learning technologies rely on large amounts of data to learn and improve performance. Machine learning algorithms cannot guarantee the accuracy and reliability of the models they generate without learning from sufficient data. Deep learning models require even more data due to their complex neural structures, and without big data, it's difficult to effectively train these models.

Without artificial intelligence technology, there would inevitably be limitations in big data analysis. Big data often includes unstructured data (e.g., text, images, video). AI technology is useful for analyzing this unstructured data and extracting patterns. Without AI, analyzing such unstructured data becomes difficult. AI excels at quickly analyzing large-scale data and discovering hidden patterns or trends. It can be time-consuming and inefficient for humans to directly analyze large-scale data. Consequently, without AI, it would be difficult to develop sophisticated prediction models based on big data analysis, and it would be virtually impossible to analyze real-time data streams to provide immediate insights.

Artificial intelligence and big data have a complementary relationship and create powerful synergy through convergence. The convergence of artificial intelligence and big data can be seen as the core of all technological convergence.

Artificial intelligence and big data technologies can be fused for various purposes in various fields. To help readers understand, let's look at some examples of fields or purposes where artificial intelligence and big data convergence is possible.

[Customer Service]

AI and big data can be integrated for customer service purposes in various fields. A representative example is AI chatbots.

Big data technology is used to collect and store data from various sources (e.g., conversation history, user profiles, user feedback), and analyze the data to extract features. To perform AI chatbot functions, various AI models (e.g., natural language processing models, prediction models, conversation management models) are trained and deployed to internal systems.

AI chatbots consist of these AI models, and when conversing with individual users in actual business, the AI models collaborate to provide solutions. After the natural language processing model (NLP) understands the user's question, the prediction model identifies the user's intention, and the conversation management model responds appropriately. Additionally, as the AI chatbot converses with individual users, it can identify individual user needs or interests and reflect this to provide more personalized responses.

[Inventory Management]

AI and big data can be fused for inventory management purposes in various fields such as retail and manufacturing.

Big data technology is used to collect and store various data (e.g., sales data, inventory data) from various sources and extract important features. To perform inventory management optimization functions, various AI models (e.g., demand prediction models, inventory optimization models) are trained and deployed to internal systems.

In actual business environments, AI models collaborate and provide solutions for optimal inventory management. The prediction model predicts future demand, and the inventory optimization model optimizes inventory levels based on predicted demand. Also, the model is improved by reflecting the difference between actual demand and predictions, and the model is updated whenever new data comes in.

[E-Commerce; Product Recommendation]

AI and big data can be combined for product recommendation purposes in the e-commerce field.

Big data technology is used to collect various data (e.g., user behavior data, user profile data, transaction data, product data) from various sources and extract important features. Based on this, various AI models (e.g., prediction models, recommendation models) are trained to perform product recommendation functions, and the trained AI models are deployed to internal systems.

In actual business, AI models collaborate to provide recommendations to individual users. The prediction model predicts individual user behavior, and the recommendation model uses that data to provide personalized product recommendations. Also, as individual users use the platform more, more personalized recommendations can be provided through the collection of behavioral data.

[Finance; Fraud Prevention]

AI and big data can be converged for fraud prevention purposes in the financial field.

Big data technology is used to collect and store data (e.g., transaction data, user data) from various sources and extract features important for financial fraud detection (e.g., transaction amount, time, location, transaction frequency). Based on this, various AI models (e.g., anomaly detection models, prediction models, classification models) are trained to perform financial fraud prevention functions. For example, the anomaly detection model detects transactions with patterns different from normal transactions, the classification model classifies transactions into normal and fraudulent transactions, and the prediction model predicts the possibility of fraud based on past data. These trained AI models are deployed to internal systems.

In actual business environments, AI models collaborate to provide financial fraud prevention solutions. When suspicious transactions that deviate from normal transaction patterns are detected, warnings are sent, or transactions are automatically blocked. For example, it can detect anomalies in card transactions in real-time to block fraudulent transactions, or monitor large-scale fund transfers to detect and block abnormal transfers. Also, the model is improved by reflecting the model's prediction results, and as new data comes in, the model automatically learns to make increasingly accurate predictions.

[OTT; Content Recommendation]

AI and big data can be fused for the purpose of providing personalized content in OTT.

Big data technology is used to collect, store, and analyze various data (e.g., viewing history, search history, ratings and reviews, click stream data, user profiles, usage patterns) from multiple users on the OTT platform. Based on this, AI models (e.g., prediction models, recommendation models) are trained and deployed to internal systems.

In actual business environments, AI models analyze user data in real-time to predict user preferences and recommend personalized content.

[Automotive; Autonomous Driving]

AI and big data can be integrated for autonomous driving purposes in the automotive field. For example, through the convergence of AI and big data, functions can be implemented to plan optimal driving routes and automatically respond in dangerous situations.

Using driving-related data collected through big data technology, AI models (e.g., object recognition models, lane recognition models, driving route planning models, vehicle motion prediction models, collision avoidance models) are trained to perform autonomous driving functions, and the trained AI models are deployed to in-vehicle systems.

In actual driving environments, AI models collaborate to provide solutions. They recognize roads and surrounding objects in real-time through cameras, LiDAR, and radar (object recognition model), track road lanes in real-time (lane recognition model), plan optimal driving routes based on real-time data (driving route planning model), predict the movement of surrounding vehicles to detect dangerous situations in advance (vehicle motion prediction model), and immediately decide on avoidance routes and execute vehicle control commands (collision avoidance model). Additionally, the performance of AI models is continuously improved through data collected during driving.

[Industrial Equipment; Maintenance]

AI and big data can be integrated for maintenance management of industrial equipment.

Big data technology is used to collect and store data logs automatically generated from existing equipment and systems (e.g., operational data, maintenance records, sensor data), and data manually recorded by workers or engineers on-site. Important features are extracted through data analysis. Based on the extracted features, AI models (e.g., failure prediction models, optimization models) are trained and deployed to internal systems.

In actual operating environments, AI models provide smart equipment management solutions. Using existing equipment condition monitoring systems, they analyze data in real-time to predict equipment failures in advance and plan necessary maintenance. This minimizes equipment downtime and reduces maintenance costs. Additionally, through real-time data analysis, equipment operation is optimized to improve energy efficiency, productivity, etc., and reduce operating costs.

[Refrigerator; Food Management]

AI and big data can be combined for food inventory management purposes in refrigerators.

Based on data collected through big data technology (e.g., images, consumption patterns), AI models (e.g., image recognition models, prediction models) necessary for food inventory management functions are trained. For example, the image recognition model recognizes what foods are present through photos of the refrigerator interior, and the prediction model analyzes food consumption patterns to predict necessary foods. These trained AI models are deployed to the internal system of the refrigerator.

In real life, AI models collaborate to provide customers with various food management solutions. For example, AI models can monitor food inside the refrigerator and, considering the user's consumption patterns, send notifications or automatically generate orders.

[Cosmetics; Skin Care]

AI and big data can be integrated for skin care tailored to an individual's skin condition.

Big data technology is used to collect, store, and analyze various data (e.g., skin data, cosmetics data, behavioral data), and based on this, various AI models (e.g., skin type analysis models, recommendation models) are trained for personalized cosmetics recommendation functions. For example, the skin type analysis model analyzes the user's skin condition, and the recommendation model recommends cosmetics based on user data and cosmetics data.

In actual business environments, AI models can collaborate to receive user's skin data and recommend or manufacture optimal cosmetics.

[Smartphone; Health Management]

AI and big data can be converged for various purposes in the smartphone field. For example, the convergence of AI and big data is possible to provide health management services through smartphones.

Big data technology is used to collect and store various data (e.g., smartphone built-in sensor data, user input data) and extract important features (e.g., user's average step count, exercise frequency, eating habits) through data analysis. Based on the extracted features,

AI models (e.g., prediction models, anomaly detection models, recommendation models) are trained. For example, the prediction model predicts future health conditions, the anomaly detection model detects abnormal health conditions or anomalies, and the recommendation model provides personalized health management advice.

In real environments, AI models collaborate to provide health management solutions to users. Based on individual user's real-time data, they can provide personalized exercise plans, nutritional intake recommendations, or detect health anomalies to allow preventive measures to be taken.

Expansion: AI + Big Data + Digital, Physical, and Biological Technologies

The convergence of AI and big data creates even more powerful synergy when combined with other digital, physical, and biological technologies.

The Internet of Things (IoT) enables real-time data collection, 5G enables fast data transmission, and cloud computing allows efficient storage, processing, and analysis of large-scale data without directly owning or managing computing resources. Blockchain increases data reliability by securely and transparently storing collected data. AR/VR helps intuitive understanding by visualizing data analysis results. Biotechnology enables the collection of more diverse data such as users' biometric information, robotics executes AI decisions in the physical world, and 3D printing quickly implements AI-based optimized designs into actual products.

Here's a more detailed explanation of how the integration of AI and big data is further combined with other technologies:

Data Collection Stage:
Big data technology is used to collect large-scale data from various sources (e.g., websites, social media, transaction records).
When combined with IoT technology, real-time collection of large-scale data becomes possible.
When combined with biotechnology, more diverse data such as users' biometric information can be collected.

Data Transmission and Storage Stage:
Collected large-scale data can be transmitted via 5G networks and stored in the cloud. 5G enables fast transmission of large-scale data without delay, and cloud computing makes it easy to expand computing resources and storage space, facilitating the analysis of large-scale data.
Big data technology is used to store large-scale data in a distributed manner, with structured and unstructured data stored in separate databases. Big data technology

is used to refine data, correcting errors and converting it into a form suitable for analysis.
Storing collected data on a blockchain can prevent tampering and increase data reliability by transparently recording the AI analysis process and results.

Data Analysis and Learning Stage:
Big data technology is used to analyze data and extract important features.
Artificial intelligence (machine learning/deep learning algorithms) analyzes the relationships between extracted features to learn patterns, thereby generating AI models. The generated AI models improve their performance through continuous learning, are then saved as files, and are deployed to **cloud services for use in actual business environments.**

Execution Stage:
In actual business environments, AI models analyze data in real-time to provide various solutions.
In particular, AI can visualize analyzed results in an intuitive and easy-to-understand form for users through AR/VR technology.
Based on the results of AI data analysis, robots can perform tasks or 3D printers can manufacture customized parts or materials.
Big data continuously collects new data, and artificial intelligence improves models through this.

Let's look at examples of how other technologies can be additionally combined in the AI + Big Data technology convergence explained earlier.

[Customer Service]

AI chatbots can be integrated with smart devices when combined with IoT and 5G. For example, it's possible to control smart home devices in real-time according to customer requests.

When combined with VR technology, users can interact with AI chatbots in a virtual environment.

When combined with cloud computing, AI model training and deployment can be executed in the cloud, improving AI chatbot performance.

Furthermore, when integrated with robotics technology, it can perform various functions. For example, in hospitals or nursing homes, robots can go around rooms, converse with patients to check their condition, and notify nurses or doctors if necessary.

[Inventory Management]

When IoT and 5G technologies are added to AI + Big Data in inventory management, real-time inventory management becomes possible. Sensors can collect inventory data in real-time, and AI can analyze and automatically execute inventory replenishment.

When combined with cloud computing, learning and utilization of AI models using large-scale data become even easier.

When combined with robotics technology, the efficiency and speed of inventory management can be further improved. For example, tasks such as loading, moving, and picking in warehouses can be automated through robots.

[E-Commerce; Product Recommendation]

In e-commerce, when IoT, 5G, etc. are additionally combined with AI + Big Data, it's possible to detect the user's status in real-time on smart devices and provide personalized recommendations. For example, if a user's health data is transmitted to a cloud server using biometric sensors, AI can recommend suitable health supplements or fitness equipment based on health data analysis.

When VR technology is added, users can receive product recommendations through virtual shopping experiences.

Combined with cloud computing, more sophisticated recommendations can be implemented through cloud-based large-scale data processing and analysis.

[Finance; Fraud Prevention]

In the case of financial fraud prevention, when blockchain technology is additionally combined with AI + Big Data, it can strengthen fraud prevention functions by ensuring transaction transparency and maintaining immutable transaction records.

When IoT and 5G technologies are additionally combined, real-time data collection and analysis become possible at ATMs or POS terminals, further enhancing financial fraud detection capabilities.

When combined with cloud computing, financial fraud patterns can be detected more precisely through large-scale transaction data analysis.

It can also further enhance financial transaction security by combining with biometric technologies (fingerprint, facial recognition, voice recognition, etc.).

[OTT; Content Recommendation]

By combining IoT technology with AI + Big Data, the user's viewing environment can be improved. For example, when a user returns home, smart lighting can automatically turn on and recommended content from the OTT service can automatically play on the TV.

When combined with cloud computing, storage and real-time processing of large-scale data become easier.

When biotechnology is additionally combined, it becomes possible to provide personalized content based on health conditions. Users' health status can be monitored through wearable devices or biometric sensors, and content can be recommended according to their health status. For example, it's possible to monitor and analyze heart rate, stress levels, etc. from the user's wearable device, recommend calming videos when the user is stressed, and provide content that can relax them when their heart rate is high.

[Automotive; Autonomous Driving]

When IoT and 5G are additionally combined with AI + Big Data, real-time communication with other vehicles or traffic infrastructure becomes possible. Real-time response to changes in road conditions or weather becomes possible, and advanced features such as cooperative driving or traffic congestion avoidance can be implemented.

When cloud computing is used, it becomes possible to store and analyze large-scale driving data, greatly improving the performance of AI models.

When combined with biological technology, it can support safe driving. Through biometric sensors, the driver's health condition and attention level can be monitored, enabling automatic control in dangerous situations.

[Industrial Equipment; Maintenance]

When IoT and 5G are combined with AI + Big Data, IoT sensors can be installed on various industrial equipment to collect more data in real-time, enabling quick response when anomalies occur.

When combined with cloud computing, large-scale data can be transmitted and stored in the cloud, further improving the performance of AI models.

[Refrigerator; Food Management]

Combining IoT technology with AI + Big Data allows for integrated management of the refrigerator and other home devices. For example, the refrigerator can interact with other smart devices to share information needed for meals, or adjust its operation to improve energy efficiency.

When combined with cloud computing, performance can be improved using large-scale data.

It can also provide health management services when combined with biosensor technology. For example, biosensors attached to the refrigerator handle can monitor the user's health condition and recommend personalized diets based on this.

[Cosmetics; Skin Care]

When IoT technology is combined with AI + Big Data, it's possible to monitor the user's skin condition in real-time and recommend optimal cosmetics or directly manufacture and provide customized cosmetics.

Combined with VR technology, users can virtually try on makeup before actually using cosmetics. This can enhance user experience in stores.

Combined with cloud computing, large-scale data can be stored and processed in real-time.

When combined with 3D printing technology, personalized cosmetics can be automatically manufactured.

[Smartphone; Health Management]

When IoT technology is combined with AI + Big Data, it's possible to monitor the user's health status in real-time through a smartwatch (heart rate, exercise amount, sleep patterns, etc.) and provide AI-based health management services.

Combined with cloud computing, large-scale data can be stored and processed.

Using biosensor technology, advanced health data such as blood pressure and blood sugar can be monitored in real-time, and personalized health management services can be provided.

Technology convergence is evolving with artificial intelligence and big data at its core. This central convergence is driving further integration of digital technologies such as IoT, 5G, and cloud computing. Moreover, it's extending to encompass the integration of physical and biological technologies, including robotics, biotechnology, and 3D printing.

This layered convergence, with AI and big data as the foundation, is shaping the future technological landscape.

<Figure 5> Technology Convergence Layer

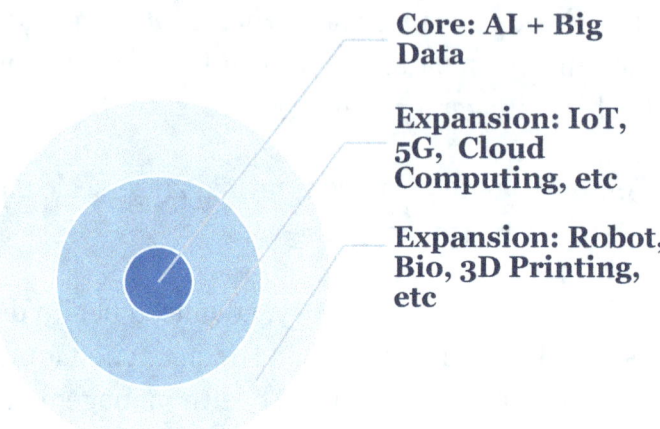

The convergence of various technologies will accelerate technological development. When different technologies are combined, it becomes possible to quickly solve complex problems by leveraging the strengths of each technology.

Technological innovation centered on the convergence of artificial intelligence and big data can be applied to various fields to advance technology and increase productivity. In particular, as the amount of data increases exponentially, more data can be used to make artificial intelligence algorithms or models more sophisticated, leading to rapid technological development in various fields.

(2) Creating Customer-Centric Innovative Solutions

The ultimate goal of technology convergence is to create customer-centric innovative solutions. This means developing new methods that can address customers' potential or unmet needs. The greater the importance of these potential or unmet customer needs, the more significant impact the creation of new solutions addressing these needs will have on customer choice.

The creation of customer-centric innovative solutions can manifest in four forms:

<Figure 6> Types of Innovative Solution Creation

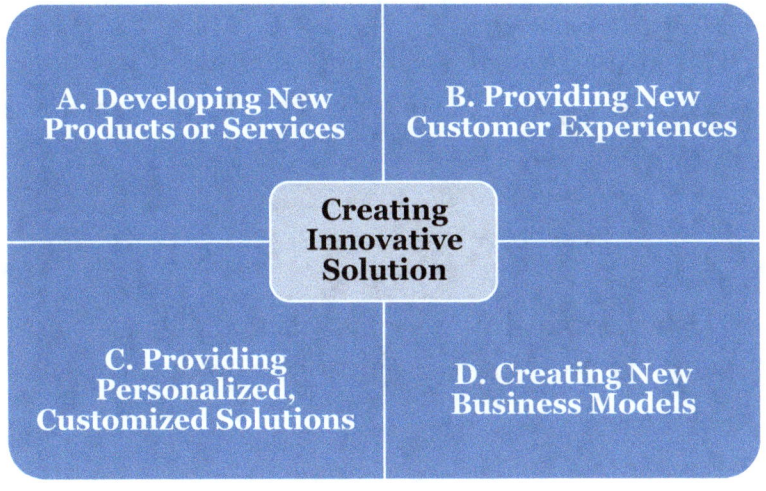

A. Developing New Products or Services through Technology Convergence:

This means creating products or services that didn't exist before, based on the convergence of technologies.

B. Providing New Customer Experiences through Technology Convergence:

This means offering customers new experiences in ways that didn't exist before.

Customer experience is a concept that encompasses the emotional and cognitive responses customers feel at all touchpoints when interacting with a specific company. It refers to all experiences customers have in their relationship with the company, including product use, service contact, and interactions with the brand.

C. Providing Personalized, Customized Solutions through Technology Convergence:

This means providing customized products, services, or customer experiences that reflect individual customer needs and preferences.

D. Creating New Business Models through Technology Convergence:

This means creating new markets that didn't exist before by providing existing or new products or services in new ways.

For example, an AI-based personalized supplement recommendation service is a new form of service (A), provides customers with a new experience (B), offers a personalized solution (C), and if this service is provided as a subscription model, it can create a new market (D).

These innovative solution creations enhance competitiveness in existing markets or secure new revenue streams by creating entirely new markets.

Let's examine in detail how technology convergence leads to the creation of customer-centric innovative solutions through the technology convergence examples explained earlier.

[Customer Service] - A, B, C, D

AI chatbots are a new type of service that automates conversations with customers and provides real-time customer support using AI. (A)

AI chatbots can provide a new customer experience by offering real-time customer support 24/7 (24 hours a day, 7 days a week), which wasn't possible with call centers or internet support. (B)

AI chatbots can provide personalized solutions to customers based on individual customer data. (C)

It's also possible to create new markets in new ways. For example, providing AI chatbot solutions to other companies can create new revenue streams. (D)

[Inventory Management] - B, C, D

AI-based demand prediction and inventory optimization, and robot-based warehouse management can provide new experiences that customers haven't had before. For example, customers can know the real-time inventory status and estimated delivery time accurately when ordering products, and experience fast and accurate delivery. (B)

Customized solutions can be provided reflecting specific customer needs and preferences. By using AI to predict each customer's purchasing patterns and demand, and optimizing inventory accordingly, products can be provided to customers when they need them. (C)

It's also possible to create new markets in new ways. For example, providing inventory management solutions that combine AI, robotics, etc., to other companies can create new markets and expand revenue sources. (D)

[E-commerce; Product Recommendation] - A, B, C, D

Providing AI-based personalized recommendations on e-commerce platforms is creating a new service that didn't exist before through technology convergence. (A)

Personalized product recommendations provide customers with a new shopping experience. For example, when customers access an e-commerce site, they can experience finding desired products faster and more conveniently by receiving a personalized recommended product list. New virtual shopping experiences can also be provided by combining with other technologies like VR. (B)

It provides personalized product recommendation solutions by analyzing individual customer behaviors and preferences. (C)

It's also possible to create new markets in new ways. For example, licensing personalized product recommendation solutions to other e-commerce platforms can create new markets and expand revenue sources. (D)

[Finance; Fraud Prevention] - A, B, C, D

Financial fraud prevention solutions are new services that detect and block financial fraud transactions in real-time through the convergence of various technologies such as AI and blockchain. (A)

Protecting customers from financial fraud provides a new experience where customers can feel safety and reliability when using financial services. (B)

It's also possible to provide customized fraud prevention solutions by analyzing each customer's transaction patterns and financial activities. (C)

Additionally, new markets can be created by providing financial fraud prevention solutions as a service. For example, new markets can be pioneered by providing financial fraud prevention solutions in the form of SaaS (Software as a Service) not only to financial institutions but also to individuals or small businesses. (D)

[OTT; Content Recommendation] - A, B, C

Personalized content recommendations on OTT platforms are a new type of service provided to customers through technology convergence. (A)

They can provide an experience where users can easily find and enjoy content that suits them. (B)

OTT platforms can analyze customers' viewing history, preferences, etc. using AI and provide personalized content solutions. (C)

[Automotive; Autonomous Driving] - A, B, D

Autonomous Vehicles:
Cars equipped with autonomous driving technology correspond to new products that add new features not found in existing cars by integrating various technologies such as AI, IoT, and 5G. (A)

This provides a new experience where the car operates itself without the driver needing to drive directly. For example, it can provide a completely different customer experience from existing driving experiences, such as being able to freely use time while driving or reduce traffic accidents. (B)

Autonomous Vehicle Hailing Service:
Autonomous vehicle hailing service is providing a new service using autonomous driving technology, mobile apps, cloud computing, etc. (A)

Customers gain a new experience of being able to travel conveniently and safely to their destination by calling an autonomous vehicle. This provides a different experience from existing vehicle hailing services. (B)

Autonomous vehicle hailing services can create a new market different from existing vehicle hailing services. (D)

[Industrial Equipment; Maintenance] - A, B, C, D

Providing industrial equipment solutions corresponds to creating a new service that efficiently manages existing equipment through the convergence of various technologies such as AI and IoT. (A)

It provides a new customer experience as customers can manage and operate equipment in new ways such as real-time monitoring, remote control, and predictive maintenance through industrial equipment solutions. (B)

Industrial equipment solutions can provide customized solutions tailored to each customer's specific needs or industrial environment. (C)

Also, industrial equipment solutions can create new markets in new ways. For example, by combining equipment and solutions, new markets can be created and revenue sources expanded through subscription models or Equipment as a Service (EaaS) models. (D)

[Refrigerator; Food Management]- A, B, C, D

Smart refrigerators correspond to new products or services that provide food inventory management solutions by combining various technologies such as AI and IoT. (A)

Smart refrigerators provide a new customer experience by monitoring food inventory in real-time, automatically managing inventory, or notifying of low stock items. They can save customers time and effort in food management and expand convenience by linking with other smart devices. (B)

Smart refrigerators can analyze users' consumption patterns and provide customized food management solutions such as personalized recipes accordingly. (C)

It's also possible to create new markets with new business models. For example, new revenue sources can be created by providing health management services combined with biosensor technology in subscription form, or by providing food consumption pattern data obtained through user data collection and analysis to food manufacturers. (D)

[Cosmetics; Skin Care] - A, B, C, D

Providing or recommending personalized cosmetics considering an individual's skin condition corresponds to creating new products or services through technology convergence. (A)

Customers receiving analysis of their skin condition and recommendations for customized products provides a new experience different from existing cosmetics purchasing experiences. (B)

Personalized solutions can be provided by manufacturing or recommending cosmetics tailored to the customer's skin condition. (C)

It's also possible to create new markets with new business models. For example, new business models can be created by introducing a subscription model that regularly provides customized skincare products to customers or by providing digital skincare consulting services. (D)

[Smartphone; Health Management] - A, B, C, D

Providing health management solutions by integrating various technologies on smartphones corresponds to developing new health management services that allow users to manage their health in new ways through smartphones. (A)

It provides customers with a new experience of being able to monitor and manage their health status anytime, anywhere. (B)

Customized health management solutions can be provided tailored to the individual user's health condition and needs. For example, personalized health advice or exercise programs can be provided by monitoring the user's heart rate, exercise amount, sleep patterns, etc. In this way, providing customized health management services can contribute to increasing smartphone and smartwatch sales by providing customers with new solutions that didn't exist before. (C)

It's also possible to create new markets in new ways. For example, new revenue sources can be created by providing health management services on a subscription-based model or by analyzing health data and providing it to medical institutions, research institutions, etc. (D)

(3) Rapid Changes in Industry Structure and Competitive Dynamics

The creation of customer-centric innovative solutions will significantly alter existing industry structures and competitive dynamics. Key changes include:

<Figure 7> Changes in Industry Structure and Competitive Dynamics

Increased Volatility in Competitive Dynamics	• Low R&D cost • Technology advancement enables customer-centric innovative solutions
Emergence of New Markets Crossing Industry Boundaries	• A market centered on customer needs emerges through the creation of customer-centric innovative solutions
Spread of Digital Platforms	• Digital Platforms can gain differentiated strengths by providing customer-centric innovative solutions

Increased Volatility in Competitive Dynamics

Generally, over 10-20 years, once-successful companies may disappear, and unknown companies may rise to the top. Competitive landscapes naturally change over time. However, it typically takes considerable time for top companies to fall or for latecomers to rise to the top.

For latecomers or new entrants to rise to the top when market-leading companies hold advantages in key competitive elements like technology, brand, and sales networks, enormous investment and risk are required. More investment in technology development, marketing, and sales is needed to secure better technology, brand, and sales networks than top companies. Moreover, since top companies continue to invest in better technology and brands, there's a risk that massive investments by latecomers or new entrants may not yield desired results.

The Fourth Industrial Revolution is expected to significantly change existing market competition.

First, the investment costs that latecomers or new entrants must bear are greatly reduced. With AI-centered technology convergence at the core of technological development, cloud services and open-source software platforms enable desired technology development at much lower costs.

Costs for purchasing and maintaining physical servers can be reduced. Cloud service providers offer computing resources as needed, converting initial capital costs to operational costs. This is especially helpful for SMEs and startups. Cloud services allow easy scaling of resources up or down as needed, preventing over or under-investment and contributing to cost efficiency. With cloud service providers managing hardware and software, companies can reduce labor and operational costs for IT infrastructure management.

Open-source software is often free, reducing software license costs. When problems arise, support can be obtained from developers through the open-source software community. With developers worldwide participating in problem-solving, issues can be resolved and functions improved quickly. This allows for much faster problem-solving than limited internal personnel. Thanks to this community support, companies can significantly reduce development and maintenance costs.

More importantly, the possibility of changes in competitive landscape increases as customer-centric innovative solutions based on technology convergence become possible. While there have been many efforts and achievements in customer-centric approaches in the past, there were clear technological limitations in data collection range, analysis methods, and business utilization. Now, with AI, big data, and various technologies combined, creating innovative customer-centric solutions is technically much more feasible. Consequently, if new competitive advantages are created through innovative solutions, the possibility for latecomers or new entrants to leap to market leadership increases.

As a result, any company with innovative ideas can provide innovative solutions surpassing competitors with low investment costs, which can act as a factor that can change market competition at any time.

Emergence of New Markets Crossing Industry Boundaries

Generally, markets are categorized by industry standards. This is why markets are viewed by industry. For example, when looking at the automotive industry, we look at the automotive market where car companies compete with each other. In the cosmetics industry, cosmetics companies compete in the cosmetics market.

On the other hand, the Fourth Industrial Revolution triggers the formation or growth of new markets that cross industry boundaries, where completely different types of companies compete.

As it becomes possible to provide innovative customer-centric solutions based on technology convergence, new markets can emerge or grow centered on customer needs. For example, based on the convergence of various technologies such as AI, big data, IoT, and 5G, innovative solutions for customer mobility needs can lead to the growth of mobility service markets or the emergence of new autonomous driving-based mobility markets. These markets transcend existing industry boundaries, and completely different types of companies like automotive and big tech companies may compete for market dominance.

Spread of Digital Platforms

Since the Third Industrial Revolution, various forms of digital platforms have emerged with the development of information and communication technologies. While they grew rapidly based on the strengths of digital platforms, there were admittedly shortcomings compared to offline channels. For example, through offline channels, customers can directly see or experience products, receive detailed explanations, and get personalized services for their needs. These are unique strengths of offline channels and limitations of digital platforms.

However, the convergence and development of various technologies due to the Fourth Industrial Revolution helps digital platforms overcome existing limitations and further allows them to have differential strengths.

Through the convergence of various technologies, digital platforms can provide customers with experiences similar to offline. For example, through AI, big data, AR/VR, etc., immersive shopping experiences can be provided to customers through virtual experiences. Also, real-time consultation services can be provided to customers.

Additionally, based on the convergence of various technologies, it's possible to provide customers with new solutions differentiated from offline. For example, on digital platforms, it's possible to collect and analyze individual customer data in real-time through AI, big data, IoT, etc., to provide customized products or services.

We'll look further at the potential for changes in industrial structure and competitive landscape through actual cases of technology convergence described earlier. Relatively smaller companies or latecomers will provide innovative solutions, causing changes in the competitive landscape. Leading companies may further strengthen their market dominance based on providing innovative solutions. The creation of markets according to new business models will also become more active over time.

[Customer Service]

KLM Royal Dutch Airlines, established in 1919 in the Netherlands, is a subsidiary of the Air France-KLM

Group. KLM provides innovative customer service by implementing AI chatbots on various social media platforms such as Facebook Messenger, WhatsApp, and Twitter. The AI chatbots support multiple languages for global customers and provide real-time responses to customer inquiries 24/7. They automate flight booking and check-in processes and offer personalized real-time information such as check-in times, gate changes, and baggage status for booked flights.

Additionally, the chatbots analyze data like customer preferences, booking history, and past travel records to provide personalized travel information.

KLM's AI chatbots are widely regarded as being ahead of major airlines (e.g., Delta Airlines, American Airlines, Lufthansa) in terms of social media utilization, language support, and personalized services. Since implementing AI chatbots, KLM has reportedly seen a significant increase in social media interactions, faster response times to customer inquiries, and a notable increase in positive feedback in customer satisfaction surveys. Theses AI chatbots handle a large portion of customer inquiries, significantly improving response times and reducing customer service costs. The automation has allowed human agents to focus on more complex issues, thereby enhancing overall service quality. The AI chatbots have also contributed significantly to increased passenger numbers and profits.

[Inventory Management]

Ocado, founded in 2000, is an online supermarket in the UK. Ocado provides fast and accurate delivery services to customers through innovative inventory management using artificial intelligence, big data, and robotics. They have a well-established system that analyzes customer order patterns to predict future demand and automatically replenishes inventory accordingly. In particular, they use AI-based robots to fully automate warehouse operations such as item storage and customer order processing, improving processing speed and reducing errors. This allows Ocado to minimize inconvenience due to out-of-stock items when customers order and enables faster order processing and quick delivery.

Ocado's innovative approach has positioned it well against traditional retailers (e.g., Tesco, Sainsbury's). Ocado has maximized its differentiated strengths as a digital platform, leading to substantial growth and a reputation as a technology leader in retail automation.

[E-commerce; Product Recommendation]

Zalando, founded in 2008 in Germany, is a European e-commerce company. Zalando analyzes customers' purchase history, search patterns, and preferences based on artificial intelligence to provide personalized recommendations. This allows them to offer new user experiences and increase customer loyalty. Recently, they introduced a ChatGPT-based fashion advisor to help customers solve their fashion needs more intuitively.

Although Zalando was a late entrant compared to Amazon and ASOS, it has been growing rapidly in the European market recently based on its AI-based recommendation system. According to a McKinsey report, AI-based fashion recommendation systems are expected to have a significant impact on consumer purchasing decisions.

[Finance; Fraud Prevention]

Revolut, founded in 2015 in the UK, is a fintech startup that provides a wide range of payment services and various financial services. Revolut uses AI to ensure secure transactions for customers. AI analyzes real-time transaction data, and if suspicious transactions are detected, it immediately stops the transaction and requests additional information from the customer. AI continuously learns to improve the accuracy and efficiency of fraud detection.

Customers have significant concerns about financial fraud when using digital financial services. By introducing an AI-based real-time financial fraud monitoring system, Revolut is gaining customer trust, which will help overcome the limitations of digital financial service platforms and enhance competitiveness.

Revolut is growing rapidly in digital financial services. The number of global users has increased dramatically in recent years, with over 30 million retail customers worldwide as of 2023, and it continues to expand its global user base.

[OTT; Content Recommendation]

Roku, founded in 2002 in the United States as a provider of OTT streaming devices, now also operates a streaming platform. Roku has built an independent streaming platform and hosts various OTT services, allowing users to conveniently access multiple streaming services through a single interface. Roku operates an ad-based streaming service called the Roku Channel, generating advertising revenue by inserting ads into the content it provides.

Roku uses artificial intelligence and big data to provide personalized content to users through the Roku

Channel. It suggests content similar to what users have previously watched, increasing viewing time and user engagement. Through data analysis, Roku personalizes and targets advertisements, allowing advertisers to provide customized ads to specific user groups. Data analysis is used to monitor ad performance in real-time and provide feedback to advertisers, maximizing ad effectiveness. Big data analysis is used to predict content consumption trends and optimize the content library.

While Roku has a cooperative relationship with OTT services in terms of hosting them, it also competes with OTT services in trying to secure user viewing time through the ad-based Roku Channel. In particular, with Netflix introducing an ad-based pricing plan, competition is likely to become more direct. Although Roku started as a relatively small company in the OTT service sector, it is strengthening its position in the streaming platform market by rapidly growing in terms of revenue, user accounts, streaming time, and advertising revenue through innovative approaches.

[Automotive; Autonomous Driving]

Waymo, founded in 2009, is a subsidiary of Alphabet, Google's parent company, that develops and sells autonomous driving technology. It leads autonomous driving technology by collecting and analyzing vast amounts of driving data and improving autonomous driving algorithms using AI and big data. Waymo is increasing its revenue in the automotive market by developing autonomous driving technology and licensing it to various automobile manufacturers. Autonomous vehicles are products that integrate advanced technologies such as software, sensors, and artificial intelligence, and the integration of software and technology is becoming increasingly important in the design and manufacturing process of vehicles. From the perspective of automobile manufacturers, they need to internalize these technologies or cooperate with companies that provide them.

As non-traditional participants like Waymo play important roles in autonomous vehicles, the market dominance of automobile manufacturers may relatively weaken.

Meanwhile, Waymo operates an autonomous driving ride-hailing service (Waymo One) in cities like Phoenix and San Francisco. Autonomous driving-based ride-hailing services will promote competition along with the growth of the mobility service market. By operating autonomous driving-based ride-hailing services, Waymo may directly compete with existing mobility service providers and automobile manufacturers entering the mobility service market. Considering that automobile manufacturers are also developing autonomous driving technology and may enter the autonomous driving-based taxi service market, tech companies like Google could compete with automotive companies for revenue pools in both the automotive market and the mobility service market.

[Industrial Equipment; Maintenance]

Bosch Rexroth, established in 2001, is a subsidiary of the Bosch Group that provides industrial automation and control solutions. It offers smart equipment solutions to various industries such as manufacturing and energy, utilizing artificial intelligence, big data, Internet of Things, and cloud platforms. Along with selling various industrial equipment, Bosch Rexroth provides real-time monitoring of equipment status, failure prediction solutions, and process automation solutions to maximize operational efficiency for customers.

Although Bosch Rexroth entered the industrial automation market later than competitors like Siemens and ABB, it has been growing rapidly.

[Refrigerator; Food Management]

Smarter, founded in 2013 in the UK, is a startup that produces and sells smart kettles (iKettle), smart coffee makers (Smarter Coffee), and smart refrigerator solutions (FridgeCam). In particular, FridgeCam is a solution based on the convergence of technologies such as artificial intelligence and big data, which can be attached to existing refrigerators to convert them into smart refrigerators. FridgeCam tracks the expiration dates of food items inside the refrigerator using a camera and allows users to check in real-time via a smartphone app. When food is running low or nearing expiration, it automatically adds items to the shopping list or fills an online shopping cart for ordering. It suggests recipes based on ingredients in the refrigerator, helping to reduce food waste and assist with meal planning.

FridgeCam provides customers with the opportunity to use core features of high-end smart refrigerators at a lower cost without purchasing expensive smart refrigerators. Smarter has seen significant growth due to cost-effective advantages and its innovative approach.

[Cosmetics; Skincare]

Proven Skincare, founded in 2017 in the United States, is a startup that provides customized skincare products. Proven Skincare uses artificial intelligence and big data to provide personalized cosmetics suitable for customers' skin conditions. It analyzes customers' skin conditions and lifestyle data to provide customized skincare products and continuously collects customer feedback and skin data to improve products. Proven Skincare operates primarily online and has recently partnered with Sephora to provide in-store experiences in some locations.

Proven Skincare has a distinct competitive advantage over traditional cosmetics companies through its personalized skincare solutions. Traditional cosmetics companies produce products for a range of skin types, but products tailored to individual users' specific needs are still limited. Proven Skincare is rapidly growing by receiving positive responses from consumers through its personalized approach.

[Smartphone; Health Management]

Apple is a leading company competing for the top position in the smartphone market. Apple provides customized health management solutions by integrating artificial intelligence, big data, Internet of Things, and connecting the Apple Health app with Apple Watch. In particular, Apple Watch provides real-time health data through functions such as heart rate, ECG (electrocardiogram), and blood oxygen measurement, helping users monitor and respond to their health conditions.

Apple has elicited positive responses from customers by providing health management solutions, contributing significantly not only to smartphone sales but also to Apple Watch sales. This shows that smartphone health management services can impact the competitive landscape of the smartphone/smartwatch market as a new competitive factor. Furthermore, it's possible to create new revenue streams in the health management service market that crosses industry boundaries.

Changes in industrial structure and competitive landscape have already begun. If data continues to increase explosively, and the convergence and development of technologies utilizing this data continue to lead to the creation of innovative solutions, the speed and scope of changes we will witness in the future will be beyond imagination.

4.2. A New Horizon of Possibilities

The Fourth Industrial Revolution brings new changes. It enables the convergence of various technologies and the provision of innovative customer-centric solutions, changing industrial structures and competitive landscapes. What possibilities do these new changes offer to Korean conglomerates and their affiliated large corporations?

Opportunities for Global Followers

Many large corporations affiliated with conglomerates are in a follower position in the global market. There is a gap with global leaders, and their market share is lower compared to the leaders. As the world economy has shifted to low growth, the growth of the global market has slowed, making it more difficult for Korean large corporations to grow in the global market. Generally, when market growth slows, competition for market share intensifies as increasing market share becomes necessary for growth. Global market leaders are in a relatively advantageous position in this market share competition. Leaders tend to have high customer loyalty to their brands and can lead price competition to maintain or increase market share based on relatively high margins or sufficient profits. In contrast, followers in the global market are inevitably at a disadvantage in market share competition. In particular, Korean large companies that maintain price competitiveness and generate profits in the global market based on economies of scale face significant difficulties. Reduced sales and subsequent production cuts lead to increased production costs and deteriorating margins. If production scale is maintained to keep production costs, it inevitably leads to increased inventory, discounted selling prices, deteriorating margins, and declining brand value.

The new changes brought by the Fourth Industrial Revolution can be a new opportunity for Korean large corporations in the follower position in the global market. Until now, it has been virtually impossible for them to overtake leading companies that are ahead in technology, brand, etc. From a long-term perspective, massive investment is needed, and considering that leading companies also continue to invest, the results of massive investment are uncertain. However, as innovation through technology convergence becomes possible with the Fourth Industrial Revolution, the possibility of overtaking global leaders has opened up. If there are innovative ideas and the capability to execute them, it is possible to overtake leading companies with low investment costs. The development of cloud computing, open-source software, etc., has significantly reduced technology development costs, and the development of digital platforms has made it easier to enter global markets. With innovative ideas, it is possible to provide innovative solutions at lower costs than before and quickly rise to a leader position in the global market. If large corporations provide customer-centric innovative solutions through technology convergence, it is possible to increase productivity and regain growth momentum. Also, it is possible to create new markets that transcend industry boundaries through technology convergence and secure new revenue sources.

On the other hand, this can also be a new threat. If they fall behind in innovation, they may quickly lose their existing market position. As companies providing innovative solutions emerge in various parts of the global market, the competition for survival will become even fiercer.

New Challenges for Global Leaders

The Fourth Industrial Revolution poses a potential new threat to Korean large corporations already holding leadership positions in the global market. If they become complacent with past success, they will face challenges from new innovators leveraging technology convergence.

However, it also presents a new opportunity. It paves the way for finding new growth engines amid the sluggish global economy. If these corporations successfully innovate through technology convergence once more, they can lead increases in productivity and drive growth.

Choices for Domestic Market Leaders

Korean large companies have high market dominance in the domestic service industry. In this situation, there was little incentive to actively pursue innovation to increase productivity.

However, in the era of the Fourth Industrial Revolution, they are also given new opportunities and challenges. Through innovation based on technology convergence, they can increase productivity in the service industry and create new demand. On the other hand, if they remain complacent in their dominant market position and do not lead innovation, their market dominance may be threatened by startups or foreign enterprises that can provide innovative solutions.

In conclusion, the Fourth Industrial Revolution is both a pressure forcing Korean large corporations affiliated with conglomerates to innovate based on technology convergence and an opportunity to find new growth engines.

The success or failure of innovation by conglomerates is directly linked to the future of the entire Korean economy. If successful, it will breathe new vitality into the Korean economy, and if it fails, it will exacerbate economic difficulties and may lead to fundamental changes in the economic structure in the long term.

The Fourth Industrial Revolution provides new opportunities for leaping forward to the Korean economy and conglomerates. However, to seize this opportunity, we must move away from existing success methods and transition to new success methods.

The transition from 'Incremental Innovation' to 'Generative Innovation' is the challenge we face. So, what specific efforts should companies make for this? We will look at this in detail in the next chapter.

Summary:

- ✓ **The Fourth Industrial Revolution enables the convergence of various technologies.**
- ✓ **Customer-centric innovative solutions can be created through technology convergence.**
- ✓ **Industrial structures and competitive landscapes are rapidly changing.**
- ✓ **These changes can be both a threat and an opportunity for firms.**
- ✓ **Innovation based on technology convergence can be a new growth engine.**

Through this chapter, we have looked at the massive changes that the Fourth Industrial Revolution will bring, and the opportunities hidden within them. We have predicted how the convergence of various technologies will create new business models and innovative solutions, and how this will change industrial structures and competitive landscapes.

In particular, we have deeply analyzed the meaning of these changes for Korean companies. The Fourth Industrial Revolution presents new challenges and opportunities for followers and leaders in the global market, as well as leaders in the domestic market.

Now we are at a point where we need to seriously consider how to respond to these changes. In the next chapter, we will look at what specific efforts companies should make to realize these changes. We will discuss the revolutionary changes in leadership, systems, and culture needed for the transition to 'Generative Innovation'.

In the era of the Fourth Industrial Revolution, we stand at a crossroads of crisis and opportunity. Our future will depend on how we utilize this wave of change.

Chapter 5. The Era of Great Transformation: A New Success Formula

The world now stands in an era of great transformation. Facing the new horizon opened by the Fourth Industrial Revolution, the question arises: what path should be chosen? This chapter aims to present the direction for Korean firms to move towards the future.

The key lies in the transition from 'Incremental Innovation' to 'Generative Innovation'. The discussion will explore the revolutionary changes in leadership, systems, and culture necessary for this shift. Additionally, the chapter emphasizes the need for an expanded role of small and medium-sized enterprises, venture companies, and startups.

Can Korea's large corporations affiliated with conglomerates succeed in innovation based on technology convergence?

To succeed in innovation based on technology convergence, new ideas and the ability to create new solutions based on these new ideas are essential. It should be possible to create new methods or solutions that can meet potential or unmet customer needs through technology convergence.

However, the innovation that most large companies have been doing so far is closer to 'innovation that improves' rather than 'innovation that creates'. In particular, they have focused on rapidly improving technology or products to catch up with leading companies in the global market.

For example, let's look at the success case of Samsung Electronics.

1. Growth period:
Initially, Samsung Electronics mainly adopted a strategy of chasing leading companies in Japan and the United States. They secured competitiveness by establishing efficient production processes and quality

management systems. They internally improved technologies introduced from abroad and thereby increased product performance and quality. They strengthened technological capabilities through continuous R&D investment and rapidly improved technology.

2. Leap to leadership:
Samsung Electronics finally leaped to become a technology leader through rapid technology improvement. In the memory semiconductor field, they came to lead the global market through continuous process improvement and technological innovation. They secured leadership in display technology through rapid improvement and new product launches.

3. After leadership:
Even after reaching the leader position, Samsung Electronics continues to improve technology to maintain global competitiveness. They continuously improve product performance and quality, increase productivity and reduce costs through continuous improvement of manufacturing processes, and continuously improve product design and user experience.

Samsung Electronics' case can be seen as a success model of 'Incremental Innovation'. But now is the time for a new way of innovation.

Large corporations were able to quickly chase or overtake leaders in the global market based on 'Incremental Innovation' and maintain high competitiveness in the domestic market. In particular, the rapid execution ability of large corporations was the most important driving force that made 'Incremental Innovation' successful.

However, they have now reached a limit. In the low growth of the world economy, it's becoming difficult to achieve continuous growth just by improving existing technologies, products, or services. The technology convergence and changes in industrial structure brought by the Fourth Industrial Revolution provide new possibilities, but it's difficult to fully utilize these with just 'Incremental Innovation'.

Transition to 'Generative Innovation'

Now, a major transformation in the way of success is needed.

We must make a transition from 'Incremental Innovation' to 'Generative Innovation'; Incremental Innovation represents innovation that improves existing products, services, or processes. Generative Innovation represents innovation that creates new products, services, or business models.

For this, revolutionary changes in leadership, systems, and culture are necessary:

<Figure 8> Enablers for 'Generative Innovation'

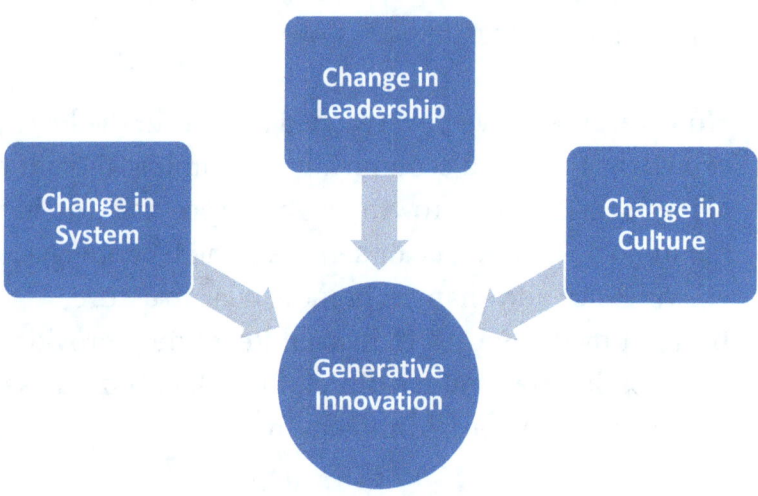

Change in Leadership

The current leadership in Korean conglomerates and their affiliated large corporations is optimized for 'Incremental Innovation'. It is characterized by owner-centered decision-making and rapid execution to improve performance in the short term. The owner decides on important matters. Owner-centered decision-making is supported by rapid execution. When the owner decides the direction, executives execute quickly. The highest ability required of executives is rapid execution. They pursue performance improvement in a short period through quick execution. This leadership exactly matches the success formula or methods so far.

Now, leadership that can present and drive new directions of change is required. For many conglomerates, what the owner thinks is very important. If the owner is not actively supportive of change, change is difficult. Most executives prioritize the owner's thoughts and follow when the owner decides. Some executives feel the need for change but are passive in pursuing it. Other executives oppose change due to concerns about organizational confusion or side effects that change might bring. They are particularly passive about new or fundamental changes. Leadership change that can overcome this is needed.

Change in System

The current systems of Korean conglomerates and their affiliated large corporations emphasize management efficiency. In situations with large organizational size and many personnel, systems are created and continuously improved to allow managers to efficiently manage the organization and personnel. Based on this, organizational managers manage the organization, performance, and personnel to achieve organizational goals. This system aligns with the leadership mentioned earlier. The leadership that emphasizes achieving quick results through rapid execution perfectly matches the system designed to achieve given goals.

Now, a new system that can motivate employees is required. Many large corporations have made efforts to refine organizational management, performance management, and personnel management. They have reorganized organizational structures, systematized organizational and individual performance evaluations, and improved HR systems. There were many cases where they entrusted projects to HR consulting firms to develop reasonable improvement plans. However, such system improvements rarely lead to active behavioral changes in employees. In fact, not a few employees in large corporations think, "I work as much as I'm paid" or "There's nothing to gain by taking initiative". Now, a new system that goes beyond system improvement is required.

Meanwhile, it's necessary to establish a data-based operational system. The reality is that many large corporations are inadequate in terms of the quantity and quality of data, personnel, and utilization. Data is so important that it's no exaggeration to say that the core of technology convergence is data utilization, and accordingly, there's a need to newly establish a management system centered on data.

Change in Culture

Korean conglomerates are characterized by a highly vertical organizational culture. In this hierarchical structure, respect for the opinions of those in higher ranks or positions of authority is not just expected, but often considered essential. There was even a joke saying, "The superior is always right". This culture aligns with the leadership and systems of conglomerates. Culture is inevitably greatly influenced by leadership and systems. For those lower in the organizational hierarchy, quickly executing given instructions is most important.

Now, a horizontal culture is required where ideas can be freely discussed without being bound by rank or hierarchy. Many conglomerates are making various efforts to improve corporate culture. Things that used to symbolize the rigid culture of conglomerates, such as dress codes and fixed work hours, have been abolished or relaxed. However, a culture of freely expressing opinions and discussing regardless of rank and hierarchy is still far off. If efforts to improve corporate culture end up being superficial, their effect will be diminished. It needs to lead to a change in constitution.

These changes will not be easy for Korean conglomerates. But without change, there is no future.

The Future of the Korean Economy

While the conglomerate-centered economic structure has led to rapid growth of the Korean economy, it has now faced limitations. The Fourth Industrial Revolution presents new possibilities, but to utilize them, a fundamental change in the way of success is needed.

The success or failure of innovation by conglomerates will determine the future of the Korean economy. If successful, it can breathe new vitality into the Korean economy, but if it fails, it could exacerbate economic difficulties and in the long term, could bring about fundamental changes in the economic structure.

Conglomerates alone are not enough. Now, the pool of firms that can create innovative solutions, including small and medium-sized enterprises, venture companies, and startups, needs to be expanded. The Fourth Industrial Revolution provides unprecedented opportunities for them. This is because with good ideas, they can create innovative solutions at low cost to increase competitiveness or create new markets.

The role of the government is important. It should prepare comprehensive solutions that can solve the immediate problems of firms with innovative ideas. It should activate competition and innovation through creating a fair competitive environment and deregulating, and strengthen policy support for creating an innovation ecosystem.

In the era of the Fourth Industrial Revolution, Korean firms and economy stand at a crossroads of crisis and opportunity.

Conglomerates must find new growth engines through the transition to 'Generative Innovation'. Small and medium-sized enterprises and startups need to grow rapidly with innovative ideas. The government should prepare effective policies that can encourage these changes.

Summary:

- ✓ A transition from 'Incremental Innovation' to 'Generative Innovation' is needed.
- ✓ Three major enablers for innovation are required: revolutionary changes in leadership, systems, and culture.
- ✓ The success or failure of conglomerates' transformation will have a significant impact on the future of the Korean economy.
- ✓ The role of small and medium-sized enterprises, venture companies, and startups also becomes important.
- ✓ The government should provide policy support to cultivate an innovation ecosystem.

Glossary

3D Printing: A technology that builds objects layer by layer based on three-dimensional design data. It's being used in various fields such as prototype production in manufacturing and custom prosthetic production in medicine and is expected to bring innovation in production methods.

5G: Fifth-generation mobile communication technology, characterized by ultra-high speed, ultra-low latency, and hyper-connectivity. It provides up to twenty times faster speed, connects more than 10 times more devices, and has ten times shorter latency than 4G. This is expected to enable key services of the Fourth Industrial Revolution such as autonomous vehicles, remote medical care, and smart cities.

Artificial Intelligence (AI): Technology that implements human learning ability, reasoning ability, perception ability, and natural language understanding ability through computer programs. AI can analyze data, recognize patterns, make decisions, or perform tasks. It's currently being used in various fields such as medical diagnosis, autonomous vehicles, and personalized recommendation systems, and is expected to be deeply involved in more industries and daily life in the future.

AR/VR: AR (Augmented Reality) is a technology that overlays virtual information on the real world, while VR (Virtual Reality) is a technology that immerses users in a computer-generated virtual environment. They are being used in various fields such as games, education, medicine, and manufacturing, and are expected to revolutionize user experiences.

Benchmarking: A management technique that studies and applies excellent cases from other companies.

Big Data: Big Data refers to large-scale datasets that are difficult to process with traditional databases. Big data is characterized by Volume, Velocity, and Variety, and the key is to derive valuable insights by analyzing it. Through big data analysis, companies can perform customer behavior prediction, risk management, and operation optimization.

Blockchain: A data storage and transfer technology based on distributed databases. It prevents data forgery and tampering by storing data in block units and connecting them in a chain form for distributed storage. It can be used in various fields such as cryptocurrency, supply chain management, and identity authentication.

Cloud Computing: A service that provides computing resources via the internet. Users can use the necessary computing power, storage space, and software through the internet. This allows companies to reduce IT infrastructure costs and increase flexibility.

Conglomerate: A large corporation composed of several different companies operating in diversified fields or industries under one corporate structure. These subsidiary companies are often unrelated in their products or services but are controlled by a parent company.

Deep Learning: A field of machine learning that uses artificial neural networks mimicking the structure of human neural networks. It can learn complex patterns through deep neural networks consisting of multiple layers of neurons and is leading innovative developments in fields such as image recognition, speech recognition, and natural language processing, especially based on large amount of data and powerful computing power. Recently, large-scale language models like GPT have emerged, showing remarkable performance in various tasks such as text generation, translation, and summarization.

Digital Platform: An online-based environment where various users participate and interact.

EaaS (Equipment as a Service): A business model where equipment is used as a service rather than purchased.

Economies of Scale: A phenomenon where production cost per unit decreases as production volume increases.

Foreign Direct Investment (FDI): Investment made by foreign companies with the purpose of participating in the management of domestic companies.

Fintech: An industry that provides new financial services through the convergence of finance and technology.

Foreign Exchange Crisis: An economic crisis that occurs when a country's foreign exchange reserves rapidly decrease.

Fourth Industrial Revolution: Refers to the next-generation industrial revolution brought about by the convergence of advanced technologies such as artificial intelligence, big data, and the Internet of Things. It's characterized by the blurring of boundaries between physical, digital, and biological domains, leading to technological convergence. This is expected to bring significant changes to industrial structures and social systems.

GDP (Gross Domestic Product): The total value of all final goods and services produced within a country during a certain period.

IMF (International Monetary Fund): An international organization that promotes international monetary cooperation and financial stability.

IMF Bailout: Emergency financial support provided by the IMF to countries in economic crisis.

Internet of Things (IoT): Technology where everyday objects are connected to the internet to exchange data. Devices equipped with sensors and communication modules are connected to networks to collect, share, and utilize information. It's being used in various fields such as smart homes, wearable devices, and smart cities, contributing to efficiency improvement and creation of new services.

Licensing: A contract where an intellectual property owner allows others to use the rights.

LiDAR (Light Detection and Ranging): A sensor technology that uses lasers to measure distance. It's used to recognize the surrounding environment in 3D in autonomous vehicles, robots, drones, etc.

Machine Learning: A field of AI that studies algorithms and techniques for computers to learn from data and improve performance on specific tasks. There are methods such as supervised learning, unsupervised learning, and reinforcement learning, and it's used in various fields such as image recognition, natural language processing, and recommendation systems. Machine learning is developing into an even more powerful prediction and decision-making tool when combined with big data.

OECD (Organization for Economic Co-operation and Development): An international organization of developed countries cooperating for economic growth, prosperity, and sustainable development.

On-premises Server: Servers owned and operated by companies themselves.

Open-Source Software: Software whose source code is open and can be freely used, modified, and distributed by anyone.

OTT (Over-The-Top): Services that provide media content over the internet.

Radar: A technology that detects the position and speed of objects using radio waves. It's importantly used in autonomous vehicles, etc., as it's not affected by weather and lighting conditions.

Robotics: An engineering field related to the design, production, and operation of robots. Several types of robots from industrial robots to service robots are being developed and used in various industrial fields such as manufacturing, medicine, and agriculture.

SaaS (Software as a Service): A method of providing software as a service through the internet.

UNCTAD (United Nations Conference on Trade and Development): A UN agency that supports trade and economic development in developing countries.

World Bank: An international financial institution that provides financial and technical assistance to developing countries.

WTO (World Trade Organization): An international organization that governs international trade rules.

ABOUT THE AUTHOR

Seung Jin Kim is an economist and business leader with extensive experience in academia and industry. He holds a B.A. in International Economics from Seoul National University and a Ph.D. in Economics from the University of Pennsylvania. Dr. Kim began his career as a Research Fellow at the Korea Development Institute (KDI), followed by a tenure as a Consultant at The

Boston Consulting Group (BCG). His corporate career spans several major Korean conglomerates. Dr. Kim has held executive positions at Samsung Group, Hyundai Motor Group, and Taekwang Group. As the COO of Korea's representative global firm, he led the entire global operation and implemented unprecedented and bold reforms in global organizational structure and operational systems. He also managed the entire business portfolio for a conglomerate as its President. Throughout his career, Kim has applied his economic expertise to various industries, driving strategic growth and global expansion.

www.ingramcontent.com/pod-product-compliance
Lightning Source LLC
Chambersburg PA
CBHW071832210526
45479CB00001B/96